ANGOLA
Hard Times
1

Chicamba

Grosvenor House
Publishing Limited

All rights reserved
Copyright © Chicamba, 2017

The right of Chicamba to be identified as the author of this
work has been asserted in accordance with Section 78
of the Copyright, Designs and Patents Act 1988

The book cover picture is copyright to SYTExperience

This book is published by
Grosvenor House Publishing Ltd
Link House
140 The Broadway, Tolworth, Surrey, KT6 7HT.
www.grosvenorhousepublishing.co.uk

This book is sold subject to the conditions that it shall not, by way of
trade or otherwise, be lent, resold, hired out or otherwise circulated
without the author's or publisher's prior consent in any form of binding or
cover other than that in which it is published and
without a similar condition including this condition being imposed
on the subsequent purchaser.

A CIP record for this book
is available from the British Library

ISBN 978-1-78623-253-3

CONTENTS

INTRODUCTION	v
KINGDOMS FROM ANGOLA	1
PORTUGUESE EMPIRE	9
BRITISH EMPIRE CONTRIBUTION	19
AFRICAN REVOLUTION	28
ANGOLAN REVOLUTION	35
MPLA, UNITA AND FNLA	42
THE FIRST DICTATOR	51
THE SECOND DICTATOR	59
THE UNITA IN THE CITIES	65
ACKNOWLEDGEMENTS	73
REFERENCES	75

INTRODUCTION

Angola Hard Times 1, will be followed by Angola Hard Times 2. I will show you, step-by-step, the events of the everyday life of the Angolan in the years before I was born and now-a-day. I believe that in sharing the hard times of my country, Angola, I am fulfilling my part of God's plan for me. The story focuses on the life of the blackpeople of Angola, who have endured an epidemic of suffering since God made the world. This history is still an important part of my life which portrays an epidemic of revolutions in the world. In the 17th century the African continent began to change by stopping the slavery of African people to the Empires. African revolutions devastated the continent and drove us to civil wars; in particular Angola, we still live in very bad times because of the consequences of the war. Angolan citizens are the witnesses to all the events that changed their culture, literature, ethnicity and mythology, to Judeo-Christian views. Imperial domination obligated those under their government to follow their literature, culture, and mythologies. This book, Angola Hard Times 1, will record our everyday life before the Empires arrived in Africa. Black people have always lived and are still living at a disadvantage, we are victims of ourselves, because of bad administration. I am sharing this history with the entire world because it is based on real life. I want to let my readers know that it is a pleasure to share my thoughts with them again. Together, we shall be a part of the wonderful world inside this book, starting firstly with kingdoms inside Angola. In chapter two will be the Portuguese Empire domination; as we know what they did to conquer Angola and its constructions. The British Empire is in chapter three, where we will learn about its contribution to the United States of America.

In chapter four will be the African revolutions; we will learn about the fight for independence on the African continent, and also, we shall discuss the strategy of the Portuguese Empire to stay in Angola. In chapter five is the Angolan revolution, where we shall learn how Angola achieved independence. Angola, was amongst the African epidemic revolution with many movements. The movements are MPLA (People's Liberation Movement of Angola), FNLA (National Front for the Liberation of Angola) and UNITA (National Union for the Total Independence of Angola). In chapter six we explore the disagreement between the MPLA, UNITA and FNLA that led to war. Chapter seven discusses the first dictator and beginnings of war, which was the responsibility of the MPLA with the influence of the Portuguese Empire. In chapter eight we shall discuss the second dictator and how he helped the country.

In chapter nine we shall discuss the UNITA in cities in 1991 and the first presidential election in the history of the country. In the final chapter, I offer my thanks to the world for a part of my life when we believed in what we were doing. Writing this book has been a blessing from God, started in heaven and shown through the books that I read. God sent his wisdom to the earth for us to have a meaningful sense in our life. This pleasure I shall give to my readers, exploring the blessing of God inside my book who we never want to miss on earth. However, I want to let my readers know that I only mention God after discussing the Portuguese Empire.

Before that, I only refer to the name of the creator of the universe because before the Empires arrived in Africa, we called God by the name of the creator of the universe in the language of Bantus. In addition, he or she is the creator of the universe before the Empire arrived in the African continent, we followed the sunlight in everyday life with excellent luck and joy to God.

THE KINGDOMS FROM ANGOLA

Everyday life of the kingdoms of Congo, Fiote, Mucubai, Bailundo, Cuanhama, Nhaneka, N'guanguela, Tututchokwé, Kimbundu and more, was jubilant and joyful among black people, because their belief was very well organized in the African continent through the connection with the creator of the universe. Thus, we can consider, the black people are the original people of the creator of the universe.

The Kingdoms of Congo, (Fiote, Mucubai, Bailundo, Cuanhama, Nhaneka, N'guanguela, Tututchokwé and Kimbundu), had much knowledge and power from the creator of the universe. They managed the spirits, souls and bodies of living beings to do what they wanted, and these skills helped them to speak with the creator of the universe. Also, they had skills to support their culture, do their handicrafts in iron, bronze, silver, wood, and excellent paintings. In this period, the people were driven by the sunlight to complete their daily routine.

Also, they spent their time following the sun in all their daily activities, they believed that the power of the spirit helped everything in their physical life. That they made rain start and stop, they followed what the spirits of the creator wanted throughout their life. In this period, amongst them were only black people and they learned from the instructions of the creator. They displayed their literature regarding their creator, and this was based on spiritual knowledge. There was an amiable bond between the creator and the black people that existed in their traditions.

They also exchanged daily experiences with other kingdoms around the African continent.

The kingdoms dedicated their heritage to antiquity, because of the connection with them in spiritual life. This power was a part of their education, learning about spiritual life, gaining skills of hunting and honing their abilities.

Each kingdom following their methods, managed to move rivers and rebuild to their specifications. However, it's difficult to understand the spiritual power used, but they celebrated their ritual by praying in the ceremonies. They gave thanks to the creator for everything in their lives, for helping their people with the spiritual power, because they had a connection with the spirit.

This spiritual knowledge in their hands was the key for life and they believed that the physical and the spiritual life should be kept together. According to belief, the kingdoms had the skills to treat any spiritual and physical disease.

Therefore, any disease was blamed on a bad spirit and prayer could cure any disease, all that was required was the protection of any human spirits.

The leaves of trees cured any injuries, they were used as were some roots. The leaves and roots were used for many functions of life, because they were believed to have a connection with the creator.

It is important to view all trees in the kingdom whether they bear fruit or not, they may have been brainwashed by the spirits of the creator.

Previously they crucified animals to perform rituals in the name of the creator, because they believed they were connected to miracles of life. They prayed in the rituals to be a successful person on earth.

Any rituals resulting in miracles, through the spirit that they believed in, had true connections with the creator. So, we cannot live without belief in spiritual power that is viewed as the same as the creator.

This ritual helped them to be successful in life, which made them believe very much in the creator and they have explored all knowledge of the creator. The new generation also explored these rituals by praying around the bonfire throughout the night.

The younger heard and learned about the culture, literature and tradition in the ballads sung by black people across the world and this was viewed as great magic.

ANGOLA HARD TIMES 1

The kingdoms of Congo: Fiote, Mucubai, Bailundo, Cuanhama, Nhaneka, N'guanguela, Tututchokwé and Kimbundu knew very well how to deal with spiritual power.

They displayed the oral traditions in all night dancing around the bonfire, the sun appearing, disappearing and the bonfire turned to ash. The new day was greeted by the people dancing.

The ceremony was full of energy, moved in the rituals and practice to show everybody the light of the creator. The rituals in the ceremonies showed that life has meaning to explore in this world, which just the weak ignore.

The ceremonies in the middle of the night during the hard times brought hope, no one worried it may disappear one day, it was more important to enjoy the moments sharing ballads around of the bonfire.

This was proved on the nights when the elders would nominate those who were strong to become chief of the kingdom. The elders observed the strong new generation and felt their own tiredness.

They were always believed and they shared the perfect history of black people. In the nights, the youngest never slept or showed any weakness, if they did; the elders might exclude them from the bonfire.

Those who were excluded from the bonfire would have to die, because the elders could say that they had bad spirits and this would remove them.

The power and practice of the rituals showed how black people lived in their kingdoms.

The sadness, the women lived excluded from their kingdoms. The kings who had no male children put their daughters as the chief of the group or queen. Then, both may be excluded from ballads around the bonfire.

Always the rituals got hot, the beat of the drums speaking any language inside the hearts of living beings, the heart understood the language of the drums that they have had good times with the creator. The elders got drunk, the youngest men were dancing and older people were teaching young women how to prepare meals. The babies cried in the nights when the ballads were sung around the fire, knowing that one day it would be them dancing around the fire. All of them felt comfort from the creator. Even though they were without a clock to know the time to go to bed, and none of them knew their date of birth, they believed they were born in the time of rain, sun or harvest.

The creator showed his love, without any confusion in their hearts, the kingdoms knew they had a good relationship with the creator. The creator knew his creation was appreciated because of the obedience amongst the kingdoms.

The people invented new skills and there was great wealth in the earth. It was the spiritual power that enabled the kingdoms to increase production in Africa.

The African continent became the home of human beings to do their research, as they travelled around other kingdoms selling their arts. The black people travelled around the world, without any intention to disturb other human beings, because they believed that the earth belongs to the creator of the universe. The knowledge of the spirit drove the kingdoms to live a good life, because they followed the sunlight where it all started and ended. Also, they were as astrologists and anthropologists in the world, because the spiritual power made them very respectful. Other parts of the world believed that the black people in Africa had too much power. They saw the mysterious power of the African rituals, and the spiritual gift of foretelling the future. This gift brought them great pleasure, as they could foresee the future as did the prophets in the bible. Every person in the kingdoms attempted to learn from the spirits how to protect themselves. The kingdoms followed the foot prints left by their predecessors in ballads, these traces were an important part of their mythology.

In mythology, they used blood, spirits, and bodies of human beings in certain rituals. Many people were dying at the hands of the kings or anyone that had this spiritual power, mixed with the mythology.

The kingdoms began playing too much with the spirits of the creator in the rituals, which changed their ways. In particular the kings, they sent many bad spirits to disturb many communities, in order to control the kingdoms. The kingdom of Congo became very powerful in the African continent.

ANGOLA HARD TIMES 1

Fights were started by the kingdoms, which increased the regional problems of tribalism and other kingdoms had to protect themselves. Any kings that were caught attacking other kingdoms were killed and their bodies, blood and spirits used in the rituals. People who were ill, hired someone who could remove the bad spirits from their bodies. The spiritual power became a very valuable and profitable business. The kings had spies among their population, and they were informed that many people had the spiritual power. Some people called them fetishists, magicians, and prophets.

The fetishists sent bad spirits and the prophets took them away from the bodies of those who had been sent bad spirits. The magician was and is still like a fetishist or a prophet, but today! In our society, they are called Kimbandeiro. Today, modern magicians separate themselves from fetishism and prophesies, maybe they avoid spirits, blood, and the bodies of people. Magicians perform in public places, like the square, to allow everybody to view and pay for the show. They have the respect of the world because of the connotation of the name, which mean less trouble in the world compared with fetishists and prophets. However, all of them sometimes require blood, spirits and bodies of people or animals, as did the kingdoms inside the Bible. The kingdoms have had too much spiritual power in their hands, and they do what they want, rather than the will of the creator. The creator saw how his gifts were being used by the kingdoms and decided to go far away. The people felt very sad when the creator abandoned them. The kingdoms completely lost their way and divided, they did not want to mix with eachother. The rituals increased, using blood, spirits and bodies of human beings to see if the creator would speak with them. Without any answer from the creator, the beliefs, rituals, ceremonies and African mythology was very badly disaccredited.

The kings stopped caring for their people and rituals continued using bodies, they thought that this would persuade the creator to return to them. The people became envious of those who had the spiritual ability and they complained to the kings about their unhappiness.

The kings stopped listening to their communities, everybody complained about the rituals. The blood, spirits, bodies and souls of the human beings were becoming useless. The population started calling the kings fetishists and magicians, because they knew that the kings were doing this just to be rich. The kings used human beings in the rituals and this became an excuse for killing people for their desire.

Kings were using the traditional rituals to kill people to increase their wealth.

The situation grew worse as many people died by the hands of the kings. The kings had many children and grandchildren, but they slept with underage women. They were viewed as big, beautiful bodies and breasts. The kings and their staff raped many children and the people believed their children were victims of the kings. The parents must obey what the kings wanted to do with their children to satisfy their spirits in the rituals. In order to survive everyone learned how to use spirits in the rituals to kill others. The hearts and minds of the people had changed and the African continent became bad.

Today, the black people just fight each other, sometimes without reason. Africa has become a very dangerous place to live. The children were accused by the fetishists, and the population believed their bodies had bad spirits and they were killed by the people in the name of the creator.

The Congo controlled many kingdoms in Africa, as we can see on the map below, the kingdom of the Congo is now modern-day Angola.

Meanwhile, many kingdoms in Africa were killed by their people, raped and sold into slavery to other kingdoms. The people were sold and sent to the north of Africa in the Arabic Empire where the rituals became beliefs, followed by many people. The kingdoms displayed disrespect for people and some ran away to other kingdoms to save their family.

The kingdoms were all the same, so some people's only option was to stay in the bush and create their own community. The tribes of Kimbundu, Tututchokwé, Fiote, some part of N'guanguela and more, have their heritage or roots in the kingdom of Congo.

EXTENSÃO DO REINO DO KONGO NO SÉCULO XVI

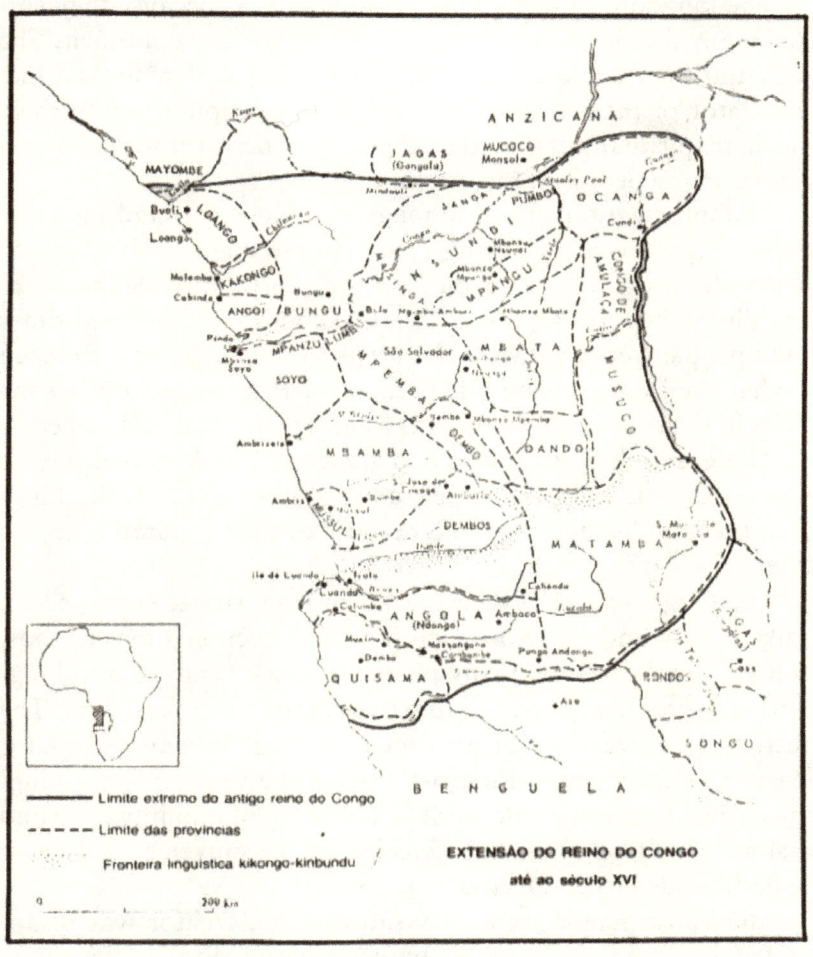

HISTÓRIA DE ANGOLA, MINISTÉRIO DA EDUCAÇÃO DA R.P.A.

The tribes of Mumuila, Mucubai, Camuanha, part of N'guanguela, Cuanhama and Nhaneka and more, have their heritage or roots in the kingdom of Bailundo.

Therefore, now-a-day all of them are called kingdoms and are; kingdoms of Congo, Fiote, Kimbundu, Bailundo, N'guanguela, Nhaneka, Mucubai, Tututchokwé, Cuanhama and more.

The kingdom of Congo became very weak, because they suffered many divisions and defeats across the African continent. The kings and their subjects practiced the rituals so they looked like the creator of the universe. The kings paid people to find others who had spiritual gifts, so that they could perform miracles and surprise many people in the world.

The information spread amongst the kingdoms and the poor people were powerless. Many black people made it their job to inform the kings who had the spiritual knowledge. Some kings were discredited during this difficult period due to the hard times as the people were annoyed. The kings forced the people to listen to what they were saying but because of their knowledge of the spirits in the rituals, the kingdoms fought to control each other.

Therefore, the people who had great spiritual knowledge were nominated as the chiefs of their communities. Indeed, the kings killed them and some were sold because of their reputation as the kings.

The kings registered their marks on iron, stone, wood, silver, bronze, ivory and more, as each kingdom occupied many lands. Each kingdom captured many people to work for them and kingdoms who had many people were considered a rich kingdom. The spiritual gifts became just an excuse to hunt human beings for pleasure, to use them in the rituals and to be very powerful kingdoms. They forgot that the spirit is a blessing of humility, love and passion, which belongs to the creator of the universe, and he or she had decided to go far away.

The black people were very sad that the creator was disappointed by them, so the creator gave permission to the white people to intervene, to stop what the black people were doing to their lives in the African lands. In particular, the kingdoms of Congo, Nhaneka Kimbundu, Bailundo, N'guanguela, Fiote, Mucubai, Tututchokwé, Cuanhama and more.

PORTUGUESE EMPIRE DOMINATION

Therefore, the problem is everywhere in the world and also in the spiritual life when the creator of the universe was forced to create the earth. As we know he or she is still fighting with his spirit called Lucifer.

However, the history of mankind says; we are on trial by the creator. The Romans or Christians called the creator of the universe, "in the name of God" and they conquered most parts of the world, before it was conquered by the Babylonian, Persian, Arabic and Greek Empires. From the 12th to the 14th centuries there was danger in Europe, due to the faithful followers of the Roman Empire and those who believed in the Bible. The same Bible that the Romans hid, once discovered this book called the bible, caused controversy due to the hierarchy in the name of Jesus Christ. They became faithful Protestants, to avoid the Romans praying to an icon, this created many disagreements amongst them. This was because some patriots believed in the Bible having the law of God that condemns praying to any icons. The European continent was the centre of many protests to reform the Roman Church. The Bible had opened the eyes of many people and thus the Protestant Church was founded.

They decided to follow in the footsteps of the Babylonian, Persian, Arabic, Greek and also Roman Empires, when they conquered the world. The Protestants started to teach the word of the Bible and this increased their followers throughout the world. The Portuguese people were the crucial factor in spreading the word of the Bible, throughout the Portuguese territory and part of Spain. During the rule of the Babylonian, Persian and Greek Empires it was controlled by the Arabic Empire. The Protestants took this chance to travel the world with the Portuguese Empire, because they were perfectly placed to make contact around the globe. Due to these events in Europe, the renaissance grew and spread throughout the entire world. The Portuguese Empire had arrived in the north of African determined to conquer the Arabic territories. However, this was almost impossible, because of the nation's strong Arabic beliefs and traditions, which wouldn't accept change. In 1492 the Portuguese Empire arrived in the kingdom of Benin and was rejected, as the current culture was roman. There was a change in attitude towards the arts and humanities, placing the individual human being at its heart. This issue helped them to have an excellent connection with the black people in the kingdom of Benin.

Jesus Christ was responsible for the cultural encounter and this contributes to our understanding of other civilizations. On account of us being all the same and created by the creator of the universe.

The black people were and still are excellent at making artefacts of iron, bronze, wood, stone and silver, and the Bible showed another direction towards the Portuguese Empire. Then, they started trading with the kingdom of Benin, this was the strategy of the Portuguese Empire to conquer the kingdom of Benin once failed in the Arabic world.

The Portuguese Empire was made very welcome and they were excellent customers of the kingdom of Benin. The black people were delighted that this showed everybody wanted to buy their arts, through the high quality and the great passion in their heart, when they made it. The Portuguese Empire was delighted with the many artefacts made in the kingdom of Benin, and they decided to explore all the African continent. Towards the south west, they arrived in the kingdom of Congo and viewed the red blood in the veins of the black people connected with their arts, and their domination was successful.

The Portuguese Empire bought and became the first customers in the European Empire of the kingdom of Congo. In exchange, the kingdom of Congo gained all the support of the Portuguese

Empire, who showed them how to fight and use weapons. They also showed them the technique of making mirrors, forks, spoons and more. This was because the black people ate without forks and spoons, just with their hands, also the black people had never seen their faces very clearly, just in the rivers or in other bodies of water.

The Portuguese Empire, successfully travelled to other kingdoms, Fiote, Mucubai, Bailundo, Cuanhama, Nhaneka, N'guanguela, Tututchokwé, Kimbundu and more. Sadly, the Portuguese Empire captured black people and sold them on to other kingdoms and in particular to the Arabic world.

Also, the Portuguese Empire started by buying black people and selling them to the Arabic world, but the American continent was the perfect place to send the black people to work. Nevertheless, the Portuguese Empire sold many black people to other kingdoms and the Congo was very angry. The kingdom of Congo controlled many kingdoms as we can view in the map below.

As the Portuguese Empire traded with all the other kingdoms, it unfortunately paid less attention to the kingdom of Congo. This caused the kingdom of Congo to fight with the Portuguese Empire, but the plan failed. The Portuguese Empire, joined with the kingdoms of Kimbundu, and established their power and office there, especially in the Island of Loanda. The kingdom of Bailundo was a big victim of slavery and they were sent to work in other kingdoms and around the world. Whilst the Portuguese Empire and the kingdom of Kimbundu became very good friends, the kingdom of Congo separated from the kingdom of Kimbundu. This blocked the kingdom of Congo from attacking other kingdoms, especially in the south of Angola. The kingdom of Congo was pushed back to the north in their central office, presently called Mbanza-Congo in the province of Zaire.

However, other kingdoms came to life and the Portuguese Empire started calling the many tribes, kingdoms. The Portuguese Empire controlled all the kingdoms and their success was heard of in Europe, and they decided to explore the African lands.

The Belgian Empire arrived in the kingdom of Congo and it joined with them, because they needed help to regain their territories that were held by the Portuguese Empire.

CHICAMBA

EXTENSÃO DO REINO DO KONGO NO SÉCULO XVI

HISTÓRIA DE ANGOLA, MINISTÉRIO DA EDUCAÇÃO DA R.P.A.

This was a very difficult time, where white people betrayed their own in favour of the black people. The Belgian Empire did nothing to help the kingdom of Congo and just explored their kingdom. The people from the kingdom of Congo had to obey the Belgian Empire and also became their slaves. The Portuguese Empire became very rich and discovered the African crafts made in iron, bronze, silver, wood and stone. The African people taught the European Empires many things. The Portuguese Empire controlled many of the African kingdoms, including:

Mucubai, Nhaneka, Fiote, Cuanhama, N'guanguela, Bailundo, Kimbundu, N'tututchokwé, part of the kingdom of Congo and more. The Portuguese Empire dominated the black people and had them sign agreements with them, unfortunately the black people had no idea what they were signing. The black people were happy to have something new in their lives and were unaware that the Portuguese Empire was deceiving them. They had secret meetings with the kingdoms of Kimbundu and suggested that they become one big kingdom. However, this did not happen and the kingdoms of Congo and Bailundo remained independent. The kingdom of Kimbundu was culpable of taking black people from other kingdoms to be sold as slaves.

The kingdom of Kimbundu attempted to protect themselves but the fighting amongst the black people increased. The Portuguese Empire found it difficult to stop them fighting and under pressure of the Protestant rule they tried to convert the black people to Christianity and stop them praying at the rituals and killing people. The Portuguese Empire, started to bring more followers of Christianity to convert the kingdoms and most of the kingdoms were reformed and the murder in the rituals was stopped. The word of the bible impressed the kingdoms and they thought it may be the will of God for the black people to murder each other. The domination was successful, the Portuguese Empire converted all of them and recognized that the black people made excellent artefacts. The kingdoms became obedient to the Portuguese Empire, their skills were appreciated. Their crafts captivated the world and changed people's understanding of the race, culture, tradition, ethnicity and beliefs of the African people. This was important for the black people; the world was now aware of their heritage. This surprised others, intellectual white people pondered how the illiterate black people had powerful arts that symbolize life.

The Portuguese Empire took the first step to introduce themselves to the world, with its culture, tradition, ethnicities and afterwards baptized all the kings with their people. However, someone had to be in charge, each kingdom attempted to do this, but were unsuccessful, they were controlled by the schemes of the Portuguese Empire. Each kingdom didn't know who was behind their fight which was the unscrupulous regime of the Portuguese Empire. The only way to escape the regime of the Portuguese Empire was to die.

From the 15th to the 19th centuries the Portuguese Empire raped women, men and children. This became the first Empire that had more mixed children than any other colony. The black people with their fetishism, prophecy, magician and more, could not stop what the Portuguese Empire did.

In addition, the black people contributed to destroying their fellow brothers and the kingdoms became close with the Portuguese Empire. The kingdoms of Mucubai, Nhaneka, Cuanhama, N'guanguela, Bailundo, Kimbundu, Fiote, N'tututchokwé and part of the kingdom of Congo were under the Jewish culture.

From the 15th to the 19th centuries, the Jewish bible style was followed and the Empire developed the infrastructure, economy and much more. The black people worked very hard in slavery, the Empire industrialized all around and was the best economy in the world. Also, they connected the infrastructure to other Empires around the African continent.

The Empire created many things such as an oil company and called it Sonangol, an airway company called Taag, and a Diamond Company called Indiama. However, it was the black people who built everything whilst in slavery, but the ideas were from the Empire. The kingdoms were obligated to learn the Portuguese language and it became the official language around the kingdoms. To be considered intelligent it was important to speak the Portuguese language and each kingdom had their names used for some territories.

Most of territories gained the names of the Empire hero and they created eighteen provinces, which are; Cabinda, Uíge, Lunda-Norte, Lunda-Sul, Bengo, Kwanza-Norte, Kwanza-Sul, Luanda, Malanje, Zaíre, Cunene, Huambo, Benguela, Huila, Muxico, Namibe, Bié and Cuando-Cubango.

ANGOLA HARD TIMES 1

The kingdoms were settled in eighteen provinces with the mixed habit and costume of the Empire. Also, the cultural encounter began as each province of the kingdom of Kimbundu was divided into five provinces. They are; Malanje, Kwanza-Norte, Bengo, Luanda and also part of Kwanza-Sul. The kingdom of Congo was divided into three provinces, they are; Zaire, Uige and Cabinda.

The kingdom of N'tututchokwé was divided into three provinces and they are; Lunda-Norte, Lunda-Sul and part of Muxico. The kingdom of Bailundo was divided into six provinces, they are; Huambo, Bié, Huila, Namibe, Benguela and also part of Kwanza-Sul. The kingdom of Cuanhama was divided into two provinces, they are; Cuando-Cubango and some part of Muxico. The kingdoms of Nhaneka were divided into two provinces, they are; Cunene and part of Huila. All these kingdoms had their descendents inside all of the Angolan provinces but the kingdom of Bailundo had the most. This kingdom had about 50% of its population in Angola and they spoke a language called Umbundu, which was the second language spoken after Portuguese. The people from the kingdom of Bailundo were forced to work on the farms around Angola by the Empire. The land south of Angola was very fertile so the Empire made this their home.

The kingdoms are split into provinces, municipalities, villages and roads, the province of Cabinda has four municipalities; which are; Belize, Buco-Zau, Cacongo, Cabinda and the capital is Cabinda.

The province of Zaíre has six municipalities which are; M'Banza-Kongo, Soyo, N'Zeto, Cuimba, Noqui, Tomboco and the capital is MBanza-Kongo.

The province of Uige has seventeen municipalities which are; Alto-Cauale, Ambuila, Buengas, Bungo, Bembe, Damba, Maccola, Milunga, Mucaba, Negage, Puri, Quimbele, Quitixe, Sanza Pombo, Songo, Uíge, Zombo and the capital is Uíge.

The province of Lunda-Norte has ten municipalities which are; Cambulo, Capenda-Camulemba, Dundo, Caungula, Chitato, Cuango, Cuilo, Lubalo, Xá-Muteba, Lucapa and the capital is Dundo.

The province of Lunda-Sul has four municipalities which are; Cacolo, Dala, Muconda, Saurimo and the capital is Saurimo. The province of Kwanza-Norte has eleven municipalities which are; Banga, Bolongongo, Ambaca, Cambambe, Golingo-Alto, Gonguembo, Cazengo, Quiculungo Samba-Caju, Lucala and the capital is N'dalatando.

The province of Kwanza-Sul has twelve municipalities which are; Amboim, Quibala, Cassongue, Conda, Libolo, Mussende, Waku Kungo, Quilenda, Seles, Porto-Amboim, Ebo, Sumbe and the capital is Sumbe.

The province of Bengo has seven municipalities which are; Ambriz, Bula-Atumba, Dande, Dembo, Nambuangongo, Pango-Aluquém, Caxito and the capital is Caxito. The province of Luanda was previously a municipality of the province of Bengo, but the province of Luanda was the capital of slavery and gained the decree to become a province.

The province of Luanda is a very small part of Angola and has five municipalities which are; Cacuaco, Cazenga, Viana, Luanda, Quiçama and the capital is Luanda. The province of Malanje has fourteen municipalities which are; Cacuso, Calandula, Cangandala, Quela, Cambunndi-Catembo, Caombo, Cuaba-N'zogo, Cunda-Dia-Baze, Luquembo, Marimba, Massango, Mucari, Quirima, Malanje and the capital is Malanje.

The province of Huambo has eleven municipalities which are; Bailundo, Caála, Catchiungo, Ekunha, Mungo, Longonjo, Tchindjenje, Tchicala-Tcholoango, Londuimbale, Ucuma, Huambo and the capital is Huambo.

The province of Benguela has ten municipalities which are; Baia Farta, Balombo, Bocoio, Caimbambo, Chongoroi, Ganda, Lobito, Benguela, Catumbela, Cubal and the capital is Benguela. The municipality of Lobito fought to be a province, because of its power in the economy as the largest port of Angola. The railway in Lubito is connected around the African continent, but still Lubito is just a municipality of Benguela. The province of Huila has thirteen municipalities which are; Caconda, Cacula-Caluquembe, Chiange, Chipindo, Chicomba, Matala, Humpata, Cuvango, Chibia, Jamba, Quilengues, Quipungo, Lubango and the capital is Lubango.

ANGOLA HARD TIMES 1

The province of Muxico has ten municipalities which are; Alto Zambeze, Léua, Bundas, Lauau, Camanongue, Luacano, Luchazes, Luena, Lumeje, Mexico and the capital is Luena. The province of Namibe was previously called the city of Moçâmedes which had five municipalities which are; Bibala, Camucuio, Tômbua, Namibe, Virei and the capital is Namibe. The province of Bié has nine municipalities which are; Andulo, Camacupa, Catabola, Chinguar, Nharea, Chitembo, Cuemba, Cunhinga, Kuito and the capital is Kuito.

The province of Kuando-kubango has ten municipalities which are; Calai, Cuangar, Cuchi, Cuito Cuanavale, Rivungo, Longa, Mavinga, Dirico, Menongue, Nancova and the capital is Menongue.

The final province of Cunene has six municipalities which are; Cahama, Cuanhama, Curoca, Cuvelai, Namacunde, Ondjiva and the capital is Ondjiva.

The names of the provinces, municipalities, villages and roads were designated by the Empire. Some of the names are from the Empire's champions who dominated the black people during this time of hardship. The black people did all the hard work building kingdoms, to make life for the Empire easy. The black people were their own worst enemies due to their spiritual mistakes across Africa. This allowed the Empire to continue catching black people to sell or work for them as slaves. Consequently the land seemed to belong to the Empire and the black people were helpless. The black people were powerless, and just watched, they obeyed anything the Empire requested. This caused fighting between the Kingdoms, the black people believed that the kingdom of Kimbundo was too subservient to the Empire. The other kingdoms were very angry with the kingdom of Kimbundo this increased tribalism and competition amongst the kings. The Empire smiled, because they already had agreements with all the other kingdoms.

The Empire attempted to eradite all the rituals executed by the kingdoms, but this was impossible, because the fetishisms and magic ran deep in the blood of the black people. From the 15th to the 19th centuries the world was taken aback by the Portuguese Empire, because it was the only Empire in its colonies that integrated with the black people.

The heart of the Empire was pure and enjoyed the black people's ballads and they also used the rituals of the spirits which increased their sexual appetite for the black women. The Empire's ideas helped to build the kingdoms and they enjoyed drinking with the black people. The Empire watched men, women and children dancing by the bonfire, showing their spiritual lives in the rituals. They enjoyed the old women teaching young women how to prepare traditional meals, how to dress and much more. The Empire enjoyed seeing the black babies crying or smiling, because they knew, that one day they would be their slaves. The spiritual power also confused the Empire, because some of the rituals were offensive. On the other hand, many people were helped and the Empire was in favour of the black people. They understood the secret key of the black people, which we have lost forever, the spiritual solutions to deal with life. So, some of the black people stopped fighting with the Empire and became their very good friends. Some of the black people did not like this alliance, as they were excluded from the rituals around the bonfire. Especially, the kingdom of Congo who were powerless to fight them, but heard them beat the drum and speak African languages. In particular, the language of the kingdoms of Congo, Bailundo, Kimbundo, Nhaneka, Cuanhama, Mucubai, Tututchokwé, Fiote, N'guanguela and many more. No one could sleep due to the rhythmic beat of the drum, and the sound of many languages spoken by the other tribes.

The Empire learned how to speak the languages of these kingdoms and some of them spoke them very well.

BRITISH EMPIRE CONTRIBUTION

The generations of slaves that were born during the 15th to 17th centuries, had suffered great pain in their lives. They fought like lions for equality and the black people in the northern American continent attempted to run away to South America. Because in this period, black people were already free from slavery. Mr. Zumbi dos Plamares was a leader in South America, he occupied an area which is now called Brazil. During this period the black people fought fiercely in the northern American continent, however the black people lived in hardship. The men who were slaves in the southern American continent occupied a place the size of a small country. All black people who attempted to run away from slavery or from their master, intended to go to the farms of their fellow black brothers and Mr. Dos Palmares. This made many white people unite and go to attack the African farmer, because he was the only black farmer at this time. Mr. Dos Palmares fought with the spiritual power from the African Continent, fetishism and magic. This prophecy was very important for their freedom, this miracle was believed to come from God! Of course, it came from God.

This spiritual power was very useful to them and the misunderstanding African Kingdoms. Particularly the kingdoms of Congo, Bailundo, Kimbundu, Nhaneka, Cuanhama, Mucubai, Tututchokwé, Fiote, N'guanguela and many more, before the arrival of the Empires in Africa. Mr. Dos Palmares, learned how to deal with the power of God, how to protect himself from the enemy and help his fellow brothers.

This spiritual gift destroyed the African kingdoms, created many divisions between them and made black people lose their way and become slaves.

In this case, it gave hope and impetus to the black people to run away from the American continent. To reach the farm of Mr. Dos Palmares, the black people had to cross many lands. The biggest problem was the sea. Mr Kunta-Kinte still attempted to run away. Sadly, most of the black people who attempted to escape were caught by their masters. They were punished and badly mutilated, Mr. Kunta-Kinte had one of his legs cut off to stop him from running away again. This situation united most of the black people in the northern American Continent, they decided to risk death because they knew the lands of the American continent did not belong to the white people Without any chance of escape, some of them became closer or friends to their master and some of them gained the statute to be free. Also, some of the slaves who were close to their master, received a European style education. This enabled some of the black people to become self-employed, because of their good education. However, in the European continent, the fighting continued because some white people wondered why the black people were called illiterate, if they could produce precious artefacts in iron, wood, silver and bronze. This shows how the African people lived their daily lives, and represents their furniture, clothes, weapons and kitchen utensils.

Since the black people arrived in the American continent in the 15th century to be slaves, there was fighting between white people, who demanded respect for the black people.

Then, all the African kingdoms came to life, particularly the kingdoms of the Congo, Mucubai, Nhaneka, Bailundo, Cuanhama, N'guanguela, Fiote, Kimbundu, N'tututchokwé and many more. They finally had the right to speak. The white people showed that there was no difference between black and white. They both eat, breath and smile, we are all human beings.

Due to the events that happened in the European continent from the 14th to the 16th centuries, this period is called the Renaissance and Reformation.

This changed the Catholic Church or Roman Empire, so the world saw a revival of the Roman culture. It was a big change in attitude towards arts and the humanities, placing the individual human being at its heart.

The black people were seen as fetishist and illiterate, but also, they were seen to produce very powerful artefacts of iron, wood, silver and bronze.

Renaissance and Reformation gave hope to all living beings and especially for the black people who had been slaves for around five centuries.

In addition, the powerful artefacts made by the black people, were the keys for the white people, to believe that the black people also had knowledge. They started to view the black people differently and treated them very well, because we are all human beings. The European trade helped the British Empire open the first British museum to the public on the 15th January in 1759. Where the black people's arts were displayed and encouraged the public to think about slavery. Also, the independence of the United States of America on the 4th July in 1776, gave new hope to the black people for freedom.

Some white people and particularly the white people from Ireland, were slaves in the hands of the British Empire. Following the fight for Ireland and pressure to be free, the British Parliament on the 25th March 1807 abolished slavery.

Duly, in 1833 slavery was made illegal in the British Empire and that resulted in the black people who were born in the United State of America being very strong. They believed that the land did not belong to the white people. However, the kingdoms of Congo, Mucubai, Fiote, Nhaneka, Cuanhama, N'guanguela, Bailundo, Kimbundu and N'tututchokwé hoped to make their dream come true.

Due to all the events that had happened, the misunderstanding regarding the spirits gift, the Reformation, the Renaissance and the United States of America's independence, this encouraged the black people to fight for their liberty.

The generation of black people born around the world and especially in the United States of America, forced some of the white people to think, what to do with them.

Once slavery was made illegal by the British Empire and anthropologists had studied their culture, the black people started winning all cases of criminality in the 18th century.

Consequently the black people became very respectable throughout the world, because they knew that the people who called them illiterate, did not have the powerful artefacts, which symbolize everything throughout life! Nobody has the full power to say the pure truth about life. The black arts gave the world contexts how we must look at human beings, that these views and appreciations etc., gave the black people the statutes.

The British Empire changed the education of the world in the 18th century and at this time some of the black people in the United States of America decided to go back to Africa.

Sadly, the African lands were occupied by the European and Arabic Empires and the British was the only Empire to accept people back. That culminated in the first black people returning to their motherland in Africa in 1842. They procured the first land since the declaration of independence on the 26th July 1847, which is now Liberia. This event gave the opportunity to the black people to fight for their lands that were in the hands of the Empires in Africa.

Then, some of the Empires like the British believed that the black people could give more of an understanding about African life in general, in their arts. This state of affairs regarding the black people, their arts and their lands forced the world to abolish slavery. The British Empire helped the new generation of black people in the 18th century, all throughout the world. Although the black people constantly fought with the Empires throughout the world, the British Empire in their colonies brought about the evaluation of the black people by the artefacts they made. From the 15th to the 18th centuries the black people and their arts were excluded, the slaves in the American continent came from different parts of Africa. Accordingly, the black people from the United States of America were the representatives of other black people in the African continent. The black people who had returned to Africa helped the other black people who had never been out of Africa. These former slaves were successful and the black people started to develop throughout the world, this was partly due to the assistance of the British Empire. Who also displayed the black people's art and culture in the British museums, this annoyed the Portuguese, Spanish, French, Italian and Belgian Empires, who thought that the Briitish Empire had given the black people a community in the colonies of Africa and they may all decide to go back to their homeland.

Then the Empires would have to return the African lands to the black people. Unfortunately, the Portuguese, Spanish, French, Italian and Belgian Empires decided to divide the African continent between them. During the 15th to the 18th century, the European Empire never thought of dividing the African continent, but due to the Portuguese, Spanish, French, Italian and Belgian Empires, this came to pass. In 1885, after a conference in Berlin, Germany, the Empire divided the African continent.

Each Empire's share depended on their agreement with the kingdoms in the African continent. The Portuguese Empire controlled many kingdoms in the African continent. Especially the kingdoms of Mucubai, Congo, Nhaneka, Fiote, Cuanhama, N'guanguela, Bailundo, Kimbundo and N'tututchokwé, this became Angola. The king was called Mr. N'gola-Kiluanje, he was the second king to surrender to the Portuguese Empire, after the kingdom of Congo. In the European continent, those who studied anthropology established that the arts of the black people were very special to the world.

The conference that happened in Berlin, allowed each Empire to do what it wanted with their colonies in Africa. The Portuguese Empire occupied all the kingdoms shown in the map below.

The size of Angolan territories in Africa is 1.247 million km^2 and this was occupied by the Portuguese Empire after the conference in Berlin, Germany, 1884-1885.

In the north west of the map, is the kingdom of Congo in Angola. From the 15th to the 18th century the Portuguese Empire tried to unite all the kingdoms. From 1885 to present day, all these kingdoms and the Portuguese born there became Angolan citizens. However, slavery still existed in Angola as this was the business of the Empires.

A DISTRIBUIÇÃO DO GRUPO KIKONGO EM ANGOLA

Fragmento do mapa étnico de José Redinha, 9.ª edição, 1975

ANGOLA HARD TIMES 1

Angola was called the Portuguese city and the Portuguese Empire, lived very diplomatically in their occupation of African lands. Some of the kingdoms, Mucubai, Congo, Nhaneka, Cuanhama, Fiote, N'guanguela, Bailundo, N'tututchokwé and Kimbundu, continued fighting to recoup the kingdoms of N'guanguela, Congo, Cuanhama, Fiote and Nhaneka from the hands of the Portuguese. They had some of their people inside other countries, such as the kingdom of Nhaneka, some of their people lived in the country of Namibia. Our neighbours in the City of Cunene, had some of their people living in the south east of Angola. The kingdom of N'guanguela had some of their people living in Zambia, in the city of Muxico in the south east of Angola. The kingdom of the Congo had some people living in the country called the Rep. Democratic of Congo, in the north west of Angola as we can view on the map above.

The Empires occupation created many divisions that separated many kingdoms and these kingdoms of Angola had to obey the Portuguese Empire. That made it difficult for the Angolan people to fight for their lands.

Some white people or should we say Empires followed the ideas of the British Empire in their views of the black people, who had lived many years ago and by their arts exhibited in the European museums. The British Museums displayed the arts of the black people, as they are the same as the white. Black people throughout the world became very strong as the British Museums exhibited the arts from the kingdom of Benin, as this was their colony.

The black people and their arts were excluded from society, their arts had never been displayed in the European lands. The black people and their arts were a scandal of the humanities because of slavery.

They needed to have some representation in the world. The understanding of the British and other European Empires encouraged the sale of the arts throughout the world. The Briitish Empire knew about humanity and allowed people to recognize that we are all the same, whatever the race or colour of the skin.

African kingdoms promoted their reputation throughout the world and the Angolan kingdoms were very happy. Due to the British Empire, the black people from Angola and their arts became respected in all lands.

The British government broke the barrier of how we must perceive the black people. The perception of many governments and artists show us that culture, tradition and ethnicity are very important in our society.

Angolan arts have been displayed in museums and they show us how mankind lived many years ago and how to live a more natural life. The white people were curious about the black people, how they sacrificed themselves to fetishism and kept their beliefs, and also their culture. That showed more diversity in life than that spilled from all living beings.

This insight changed society throughout the world, and sparked the desire, to get to know more about the background of the black people's crafts, displayed in the museums of the world. This was a great moment for the black people, their crafts displayed in the museums, still attracted an audience. This caused the realization that black people are intelligent too. This increased the popularity of the black people throughout the world, especially with the United States of America, where the black people first gained the power to support their brothers around the world.

Slowly, some of them became very important people in the world, which had a great impact on the black people fighting in Angola.

The Portuguese Empire was still catching black people to sell and they also excluded them from Angolan society. Consequently, the black people in the world fought intensively for freedom.

The British Empire with their colonies and especially the United States of America made the greatest change in the world.

The Angolan black people had the belief that they could recoup their lands and the Portuguese Empire was afraid. Slowly the black Angolan people began to assert their rights to speak about their lands. The offspring of the Portuguese Empire born in

Angola, decided to go to Portugal. They would be poor people, because it is difficult to start afresh in a new country. Many white people born in Angola knew nothing about Portugal and didn't want to go, so they established themselves in Angola.

AFRICAN REVOLUTION

African revolution was a part of the world revolution and clearly showed that the blessing of God was on our side, and we gained the wisdom of nature. The British Empire played a great role when they supported the black people around the world. Its contribution was absolute, because it had a connection with the multi-cultural sharing of lives. The black people started to have the right to speak about the faith we feel in our hearts. The British colonies and the United States of America gave a helping hand, because there was and still is an understanding of black people in the world. Many centuries ago, in the north of Africa during the Arabic Empire, there was sexual congress between the Arabs and the black people. Sadly, the black people disappeared, the mixed race people did not consider themselves black and did not want to fight. This side of Africa is called white Africa and the few remaining black people had less power to fight for their lands. As there could be two different fights, this complicated the African revolution, the fight to reclaim the African lands was just in places where there were many black people.

The black people challenged the Empires and this gave them the capacity to reclaim their lands, and they fought without fear to recoup their territory. This forced the Empires to reconsider. The Empires only livelihood was buying and selling black people, this had to stop! They had to leave the black people to be free, and this was a big issue amongst them.

The Portuguese, Italian, Spanish, French and Belgian Empires, blamed the British Empire for giving too much freedom to the black people.

They are still blaming them today along with the United States of America. In the 17th century the pressure of the anthropologists forced them to stop doing what they did with the black people. Thus, the black people in the United States of America had and still have an excellent relationship with the white people. As a result, they became the first place in the world to be a multi-cultural centre. When the world was controlled by the Babylonian, Persian, Arabic, Greek and Roman Empires, maybe we believe the history of Daniel, from the bible, when he had a dream in the kingdom of Babylonia. Whatever the meaning of the foot in the dream, there became an epidemic of revolution around the world.

Many black people in the world, tried their best to do something to help other black people who did not have a voice. This culminated with Sir Edward Wilmot Blyden who founded West African Nationalism in 1901 in London, to represent the black people.

The epidemic of revolution spread throughout the African land, this surprised many Empires, and they tried to reverse the situation. But the matter of contention was out their control, giving basis to the anthropologists that we are all human beings.

Nevertheless, when all the arts of the black people emerged, there was competition for these items in the museums around the world. We believe that everything has a reason and this was the reason to understand other human beings, who have suffered in the world.

In particular, the black people from Angola, boosted the culture encounter in the United States of America and increased pressure in Angola, for the Empire to change the way they ruled their colonies.

When the United States of America changed the law of the world, the black people in Africa started to have dreams of reclaiming their land. Then, Christian education became the hub of the black people.

Christianity no longer supported slavery, this was very good news for the black people. This changed the way the Empires treated them. The black people in Africa were very happy when the south of Africa became a country. In 1910 South Africa gained independence, unfortunately, this independence was just for the white, Asian and Arabic people. It was not for the black people at this time.

South Africa became a country, but independence was the goal of mankind. In African lands during the 19th century the blood of the black people boiled in their veins. God was back on our side after millions of years, he was angry and abandoned us, because of our misunderstanding with his spirit. God returned with full power to stop the Empires killing their fellow human beings.

The epidemic revolution in African lands mixed with the cries and rituals, spilled into the heart of mankind. The Empires had to think about their future in Africa. This was perfect in the eyes of God, viewing other colonies becoming the free country called Egypt. Egypt, gained independence on the 28th February 1922. Again, this independence was just for the Arabic or Asian people who occupied the north of Africa, millions of years ago. The Empires were aware of the reduction in numbers of the black people, and this culminated in another place to be free, called Ethiopia, that never was considered colonized.

The African revolution helped them to become independent on the 5th May 1941.

The greatest outbreak appeared in Libya, they gained independence on the 24th December 1951. Once again this did not include the black people, because they were very sparse in this area.

The revolution continued with the Sudan on the 1st January 1956 and Tunisia on the 24th March 1956. This was not for the black people as they had been eradicated millions of years ago.

This had never been seen before in the world, the blood of the black people was boiling in the African lands. The black people were very angry with their masters, because the Arabic, Jewish, Greek, Buddhist, Roman and European Empires occupied their lands.

During this fight for Africa, Angola was participating but without any success, they just watched other countries getting their independence. This achievement was tremendous for the black people, none of the Empires were able to stop the greatest plague called "independence" in the world.

The primitive people carried the hunger for freedom in their veins, and this passion affected all living beings especially in Africa. The Portuguese Empire enclosed some of their domain and this colony became Guinea-Bissau on the 24th September 1973. This area had many black Angolan people and they became citizens of Guinea-Bissau. After Guinea-Bissau became a country, all the Portuguese colonies relaxed and that gave Angola a chance. They had attempted freedom many times but without success, the black people in Angola fought passionately Please believe that in this period we decided to risk our lives for our lands, and the kingdoms united.

During the revolution for the African continent, the horde of people from the Empires returned to Europe. The European lands were very small and could not accommodate them all.

The Empire generation who were born in Africa were rejected by the other white people in Europe. This situation forced the first and second world wars, because European land was occupied by the Jewish Empire.

This outbreak of revolution astonished the world and particularly the African continent. The everyday life of the black people was much worse, because of slavery, which forced them to claim the country.

The Empire sent many black people to prison without reason, black people living in their native land were very worried. The Empire never thought that one day they would leave the African lands after five centuries of occupation.

The Empires watched other Empires leave Africa. The Empires lamented their lost colonies and the Portuguese Empire planned many strategies to stay in Angola forever. People would rather die than leave, they wanted to stay in Angola where they belonged. Dissidents started to appear, and they fought against the Empire, however, they were part of the Empire too. This showed the Angolan black people that some white people disagreed with what the Portuguese were doing. Indeed, this strategy was successful and it appeared that many white people from the Empire claimed the country too, in the name of the black people. Because some of them were born in Angola, they wanted the Portuguese Empire to leave. However, they are part of the Empire too! They had experience of war, as they searched for black people for slavery. Some white people had mixed children with black women, therefore they were ideal for us to trust. The black people had parents and friends who were white and they supported the dissidents in the Empire. More white people left the Empire to unite with the dissidents and they fought for the Empire to leave their land. Of course, Angola was and still is their land of birth. Sadly, this was a plan concocted by the Empire to confuse the black people.

In Angola white people fought on the side of the black people. So, which white people? It was very difficult to know, because the strategies of the Empire confused many people in Angola. This was life in Angola, the Empire was always plotting and the black people were still fighting. The Empire was determined to stay and nothing would stand in their way, including murder.

The Empires used religion, together they made many plans, because from the 15th century to present day the Empire had remained in the Catholic Church. The black people were subservient to the Empire, they prayed to God that he may change their lives. As a consequence, the white people inside the Catholic Church spied on all the black people.

Also, the Catholic Church was responsible for the education in their colonies and particularly in Angola, the black people wanted and still want, a good education. Since the arrival of the Empire in the 15th century, the black people had received excellent educations. However, there were those in the Empire who spied on the black Angolan brothers to see what they were doing and thinking.

Many black parents worked as spies, to fulfil the need of the Empire in Angola, there were those who were of mixed race and they had received a better education by the Catholic Church.

This allowed many Angolan black people who were enrolled in the Catholic church, to have the chance to send their children to schools, colleges and universities in Portugal. Maybe some day they can go on to become priests, as many Angolan black people were allowed to go to Portugal and complete their studies. Many children knew their parents woke up very early in the morning to go to work, but had no idea what their parents were doing. Unfortunately, many children never knew what their parents did, all they saw were the black people in trouble, being dragged into their bedrooms and maybe killed. Someone had informed the Catholic Church that the Angolan black people had been fighting against the Empire. Consequently, the Empire went to every home very early in the morning to arrest them, this embarrassed many black people, so, many of them went to study in Portugal, to avoid the hard times of this country. Among them were the following people, who were very well known in our society; Dr. António Agostinho Neto, Jonas Malheiro Savimbi and Holden Álvaro Roberto.

Dr. Holden Álvaro Roberto, had the opportunity to study in the Belgian Empire by the Catholic Church. The three of them lived among black Angolans, in a community out of Angola, with the promise of getting a good job when they returned to their country, as their parents had influence with the Catholic Church in Angola. Their parents were respected by the black community as they were followers of the Jewish style of the bible.

In this period, we believe that they spied on other black people for their children to have the statute, however everybody wanted to have good things in life. When they returned, they worked for the Empire's companies and farms in Angola, but, they never worked for the government. At this time, it was impossible, the Empire and the Catholic Church would not allow it. They continued to stay among the black people and control Angola.

The Empire understood its nation and they believed they could control Angola and everything would belong to them. The astute reasoning of the Empire and their will to protect their people pushed them to invent the following: Sir Mario Pinto de Andrade, a white person, created the movement called MPLA (Popular Liberation Movement of Angola), founded on the 10th December 1956. With deep sadness, we the black people fought for the freedom of our country, but without anyone on our side.

In Angola, many movements appeared and disappeared, the MPLA fought to swallow most of them. The MIA (Movement Independence of Angola), MINA (Movement National Independence of Angola) and many more, became part of the MPLA

The black people just followed the fight without any strategies to benefit themselves and in the MPLA there were many Empire people. Nevertheless, the creation of the MPLA, was a very successful strategy to protect the Empire's place in Angola. They attempted to do what had happened in South Africa with independence just for the white people. This was impossible, as during the 15th to the 19th centuries, the Portuguese Empire had fraternized with the black women and produced mixed race children. As a result, the MPLA became a movement for the black, white and mixed-race people, so, the strategy used for South Africa, failed.

The Empire convinced many black Angolans to enroll in the MPLA, they believed they were fighting for all Angola, but they weren't. The MPLA just fought to keep the Empire in Angola. The revolution in Angola became the battle of the white people and in Portugal it was backed by the Catholic Church.

The next strategy of the Empire and MPLA was to include the colony of São-Tomé & Principe, Cabo-Verde and Cabinda to be part of Angola. The colony of Cabinda was recognized as part of Angola on the 26th May 1956, but the colonies of São-Tomé & Principe and Cabo-Verde declined. They viewed Angola to be too far from them but they supported each another in the African revolution, the spirit was just for support and nothing else. So, the strategy to include São-Tomé & Principe and Cabo-Verde as part of Angola failed.

The Empire had the experience to look after themselves and they took any opportunity to distract the black people. Their plans came to fruition because the black people were naïve.

The Empire believed that its generation born in Angola, would one day unite with Portugal to enable them to continue controlling Angola.

ANGOLAN REVOLUTION

From the beginning of time, the kingdoms of Mucubai, Nhaneka, Cuanhama, N'guanguela, Fiote, Bailundo, Kimbundu, N'tututchokwé and Congo, wanted freedom from their oppressors. In the 15th century their situation became more complicated by the arrival of the Empires. Each generation in the kingdoms had their own specific revolution and in the 19th century after many colonies had gained their independence, Angola consistently battled the might of the Empire. Without success, we just watched the death of our black brothers in the fight that caused many to flee the area. To move to the safety of the independent countries was the key. It was time to pressurize the Portuguese Empire, so we joined forces with other colonies; Mozambique, Cabo-Verde and São-Tomé & Principe. Many Angolans lived in Portugal and the black people were under the control of the Portuguese Empire.

The writer Dr. António Agostinho Neto, chronicled the Angolan affairs in poetry, during these difficult times. The world could empathize with the Angolan black people in prison. His poems flowed like a river into the sea, promoting the idea to claim our country back from the Portuguese.

Mr. Neto's wife was white and she had great influence with the Portuguese Empire. With her influence, Dr. Neto enrolled in the MPLA, which was an excellent strategy and the greatest achievement in the history of Portugal. She helped her husband to escape and surface in Africa in the MPLA base.

Dr. Jonas Malheiro Savimbi, in Portugal, engaged in the GRAE and was led by Dr. Holden Álvaro Roberto in the

Democratic Republic of Congo. Dr. Savimbi, was the secretary of the GRAE in Paris, France.

Dr. Roberto, was surprised by Dr. Savimbi, because he had many European passports and he travelled around the world easily. Portugal promised anything to still control Angola. For Angola to become independent, it needed to put someone black as the leader of the MPLA. Dr. Neto, was very confident that the black people followed him without an idea of what the Portuguese Empire thought.

The black people just supported the MPLA without any idea of what was going on in the background. Many black people were sent into slavery in different parts of the Portuguese colonies in Africa. Some were sent back to the land of their past, Angola, and especially the people from the colonies of the São-Tomé & Principe and Cabo-Verde.

Among them were the parents of Eng. Jose Eduardo dos Santos, all their children came from São-Tomé & Principe and settled in Luanda in the village of Sambizanga. This village was the home of many immigrates and people came from all cities of Angola. Anyone looking for an opportunity in life, went to work in Angola, especially in Luanda. But, they were forced to participate in the African revolution and to join the MPLA, which was still known as the immigrant movement.

The white and mixed-race people travelled throughout Angola, performing their campaigns and the Portuguese Empire never thought that other white people were fighting against them. But, if any black people walked around, the army of the Portuguese Empire would stop them and ask for their passbook and if they were allowed to be there. Maybe they were from the GRAE, because most black people, during these difficult times, were from the Kingdom of Congo. The Angolan people in Portugal, felt very sad about what they had heard on the radio and television regarding their homeland, Angola. The murder and imprisonment of black people, shocked the many Angolans in Portugal. This forced many black people to leave Angola and move to other countries. Sr. Difuila and Eng. José Eduardo dos Santos, were very surprised to hear and see Mr. Lara speaking about Angola, the message

Mr. Lara gave, was just for the white people. As a result, the black people were controlled by the white and mixed-race people, who ran the MPLA.

The MPLA trained the black people to fight against the Portuguese Empire. They also captured many black people and sent them to prison in Angola and also to other countries such as Cabo-Verde and São Tomé & Principe. The prison in Cabo-Verde was more prominent and the Portuguese Empire separated many families and made them fight each other. More black people died in Angola, by the hands of their fellow black brothers, compared to the white people.

The Democratic Republic of the Congo supported the GRAE, they were the first to become independent. All the members were black people and most importantly they were from the Kingdom of Congo. This is the same kingdom we have in the north west of Angola, and Mr. Mabutu Seko had plans to introduce Angola to the GRAE. The black people attacked many places occupied by the Portuguese Empire, the farms, the police station and much more.

The MPLA and the GRAE claimed these attacks.

The black people from the kingdom of Congo in Angola, created the movement called; UPNA (Union Popular for North of Angola). Why just for the north of Angola, if we are all fighting for the same cause?

This was due to tribalism and it was condemned by the world, so it was closed and another movement started, called UPA (Union Popular of Angola).

The UPA was more radical, tribalist and was the movement that retaliated to all the attacks made by the Portuguese Empire. They didn't care, they attacked all black people who supported the Portuguese Empire.

On the 4th February 1961, the Portuguese Empire killed the black people who complained about the conditions of workers in the province of Malanje. This murder is now called the "murder of the Baixa of Cassanje".

The UPA, was the only movement that avenged this murder, they killed anyone in sight, whether black, white, adult or child. Most of the people killed were from the kingdom of Bailundo, the

Portuguese Empire had sent them to work on their farms in Northern Angola.

The UPA killed anyone, but the Portuguese Empire just killed black people and not their own.

The UPA were criticized and called tribalists and this situation affected the kingdom of Congo. The whole world deplored the senseless killings. After they had killed their victims, they cut off their heads and used them as a ball, they then put the heads on a stick to show everyone what they had done. However, the Portuguese Empire never showed the bodies of the black people they had killed, they knew what the impact could be. The responsibility for the murders was judged in the Congo Brazzaville, by international law. No one was present from the Portuguese Empire. The kingdom of Congo in Angola, received much criticism around the world, because of tribalism.

Mr. Roberto, to save the dignity and reputation of the kingdom of Congo, closed the movement called GRAE and the movement of UPA . In 1961, Dr. Roberto, to protect his kingdom, founded another movement called FNLA (National Front for the Liberation of Angola). The people of the kingdom of the Congo in Angola, decided that it was imperative that the Portuguese Empire should leave Angola. Dr. Savimbi left the GRAE, due to the tribalism against the people from Southern Angola. Dr. Savimbi, tried to enroll in the MPLA, but was rejected, this was because he had been in the GRAE.

Mr. Savimbi, went back to where he came from, as life says "if you lose the way, think where you come from to see where you are and where you are going". Mr. Savimbi disappeared in despair. However, the MPLA and FNLA, claimed any attack made on the Portuguese Empire. The population were even more determined to force the Portuguese Empire to leave the country.

On the 25th May 1963, the OAU (Organization of African Unity) was founded in Addis Ababa, Ethiopia. The OAU, respected the FNLA, because most of the members were black people. Most of the MPLA were white and they wanted to save the wealth of their parents, which the black people of the MPLA were unaware of.

ANGOLA HARD TIMES 1

The Portuguese sent their spies to the Democratic Rep. of Congo and they tried to stop the MPLA and FNLA. The spies led by Almirante MR Coutinho, were caught by the army or intelligence of the Democratic Republic of Congo. Mr. Coutinho, spent some time in prison, the Portuguese negotiated for his freedom. The MPLA helped in this negotiation with the Democratic Republic of the Congo and they gained freedom.

The Portuguese naval prisoners were welcomed by the MPLA, because of the white people in the organization. As a result, the MPLA moved to the Democratic Republic of the Congo, in Léopoldville, now known as Kinshasa.

The Democratic Republic of the Congo, gave full support to the FNLA, because they were like-minded.

Mr. Roberto was a man who enjoyed his life in Kinshasa, with lots of luxurious cars bought from America. The world witnessed the black people dying in the war and their leader enjoying his life, however, that's life! When someone dies, others smile, the MPLA lost their way, due to the FNLA in the Democratic Republic of the Congo. The MPLA almost disappeared from Congo Brazzaville. The MPLA had the full support of the Soviet-union and Cuba, and the revolutionary internationalist Che-guevara, was sent to Congo Brazzaville to help them. Mr. Che-guevara knew all the revolutionary people in this time and he believed that the FNLA had more purpose in its fight. In 1964 the former leader of Congo Brazzaville, Mr. Massemba-Débat, planned to betray the MPLA. He attempted several times to unite Mr. Che-guevara with Dr. Roberto, leader of the FNLA, but, Dr. Roberto refused to talk with Mr. Che-Guevara. He said, "I am a nationalist and not an internationalist like Mr. Che-Guevara".

Mr. Che-guevara, advised Dr. Neto, to unite with the Angolan black people, because it was the only way for the Angolan nation to be strong. Otherwise, the Angolan people would suffer greatly, however, Mr. Guevara knew about revolution.

The Portuguese Empire, knew his aim was to help the nationalists or the black people in Angola, but the words of Mr. Guevara were misunderstood. The MPLA was an international movement in Angola and trained many black people around Africa how to fight for them. The MPLA was connected with the Soviet Union and Cuba, and Mr. Guevara's idea to unite the black people of Angola, cost him his life. The Portuguese Empire knew that if the MPLA lost, they would also lose their fortune in Angola.

On the 13th March 1966 Dr. Savimbi publicly announced his movement called UNITA (National Union for the Total Independence of Angola).

Dr. Savimbi created his movement for the whole of Angola, because the MPLA were just for the white people. The FNLA were for the black people, but mainly for those who lived in the kingdom of Congo. Throughout the world, each community had their representatives and Dr. Savimbi acted for all of Angola but especially for the south who had been left behind.

Sadly, the MPLA, FNLA and UNITA started to fight each other and forgot their fight against the Portuguese Empire. This state of affairs was very embarrassing and difficult to comprehend. This was why Mr. Guevara attempted to avoid Angolan society. This appalling mistake was highlighted amongst the Angolan nationalists. Furthermore, we heard that Mr. Guevara had died, it was unbelievable that the great experienced revolutionary man died in such a way. Mr. Guevara, was betrayed by his fellow friend Fidel Castro, in the name of the Soviet-union.

Because he tried to unite the Angolan black nationalists, he was killed. The FNLA, UNITA and also the black people inside the MPLA became useless to the Portuguese Empire. Each movement fought to be the most powerful, because of the protagonist of each respective movement. However, the FNLA was supported by the United States of America. The MPLA was supported by Cuba and the Soviet-union and UNITA was supported by the Republic of South Africa, the Republic of China and also the United States of America. So, the Portuguese Empire was involved in every movement, hoping to be the primary leader of Angola. As a result, our lives were chaotic, in the midst of communism, socialism and capitalism.

We tried to remove the Portuguese Empire from Angola but at the same time supported the FNLA, UNITA and MPLA. This was unbelievable, maybe it was the power of the spirits that had destroyed us again. The black people never learned, this generation was still making the same mistakes and living with the consequences from the past. Particularly, the kingdoms of; Mucubai, Nhaneka, Cuanhama, N'guanguela, Bailundo, Fiote, Kimbundo, N'tututchokwé and Congo, which formed Angola.

MPLA, UNITA AND FNLA

The FNLA, UNITA and MPLA, swallowed many other movements, because they were well thought of by the population. The Empire army was very afraid when they were challenged by the movements.

They didn't know what to do with these three movements and with the population who were attacking everywhere. The population attacked persistantly, the movements appeared as the mediator, to deal with the Empire. Dr. Savimbi made a very successful attack on the Empire bases and killed many of the Empire's soldiers. Portugal never forgot the deaths of their soldiers. The former Cuban leader; Fidel Castro, said to the former leader of the MPLA, Dr. Neto, "don't worry this movement called UNITA are peasants and they cannot escape anyway".

Fidel Castro said that, because the UNITA only had between one and two years experience, with less power than the MPLA and FNLA. The MPLA had more experience of political life, due to the Empire's domination of the black people since the 15th century.

The FNLA worried the MPLA, because the kingdom of Congo supported them. Each movement promoted their parents and friends, to a high position.

It was not important whether their parents had experience or not, they were still given a position of importance. Many parents in the MPLA were called Military General and still are today, if the leaders had no family or friends, the members were just general staff. If you were not nominated, it was very difficult to rise through the ranks to a high position. Inside the MPLA the white and mixed-race people had the high positions, they were chosen by the Empire to protect the richness in Angola. At this time, there was no chance for the black people to become rich or millionaires. The black people fought to be the first Angolan to be rich and it depended on which movement was favoured by the population. The black people were well-known by the MPLA, the Empire or white people who were very rich and the lords of Angola, had political experience and were well organized. Any black people on their side had more chance to be accredited, but the FNLA and UNITA didn't have any political experience and were disorganized.

The Empire had controlled the black people since the 15th century, formed Angola in the 18th century and when they became the MPLA, no one could challenge them.

Because the economy was in their hands and any movement could win, they depended on the Empire's experience. The FNLA and UNITA just watched as the populace claimed the country, without any idea what to do, some black people supported the MPLA just to be promoted.

The Empire's army had suffered a great defeat in their colonies, and particularly in Angola. The three movements amongst the population lay claim to the country. The community was determined to oust the Empire from their country. The Empire just watched as their bases were attacked by the community or one of the three movements. In Portugal, the parents of the soldiers fighting in the colonies, demanded their return, before they were all killed. They were very angry with the regime of Mr. Salazar.

Mr. Salazar was very disrespectful to his people in Portugal and the colonies were very unhappy with his regime. The concern spread around the world because of the things the Salazar regime stood for.

The Portuguese citizens also disagreed with his regime in Portugal and many of them left the country. They organized campaigns throughout Europe and they prayed for the Salazar rule to end, as a result, Portugal have always had events and displays to show their unhappiness with the discord in Angola.

The pressure increased, the Empire's army refused to die in the colonies, which they had divided. Those soldiers supported the

Salazar regime in Portugal and they started to kill many black people, put them in prisons and send them to prisons in other colonies. Capitalism started to grow rapidly and the United States of America showed them the benefits. Many countries started to accept capitalism and this changed regulation, which in Portugal increased the events. The heart of Mr. Salazar couldn't accept defeat and he died, but some of the soldiers close to him refused to tell the truth to the rest of the army. They were unaware that Mr. Salazar had died a month ago. When the army discovered the truth, some of the chiefs were very angry with his government, the military disagreed with the Salazar regime and this caused the Carnation Revolution in Lisbon, Portugal on the 25th April 1974. This defeated the Salazar regime and helped the rest of the colonies in the African continent. Particularly in Angola, after seeing what had happened in Portugal, the three movements began to panic and forced the Empire's army to make a decision. Angolan prisoners in Terrafal, watched the army staff approach them with sad faces.

Each prisoner asked themselves what was happening. Without any idea of what had happened in Portugal, the prisoners were afraid. The staff were also afraid to give the prisoners the news about the death of Salazar, they thought they might attack or even kill them, because the prison staff felt very disappointed with Portugal. The prisoners were controlled by the sad faces and silence of the guards. The staff looked at each other and waited for someone else to break the news to the prisoners of what had happened in Portugal. The prisoners thought, that today they would all die, because of the look on the faces of the guards, who found it very difficult to say the words. Or let's say they didn't know how to break the news that Mr. Salazar was no longer with us. The prisoners waited in silence and consusion, then the chief of prison took the responsibility of informing them of the death of Mr. Salazar and that they were all free. None of the prisoners could believe that they were free, because the Salazar regime had been very bad. They never dreamt this day would ever happen, but for God, nothing is hard or impossible.

The prisoners took a very long time to understand that it was true, they were free, and also to understand what had happened in

Portugal. Angolan prisoners hoped to go back home and see their parents, but they felt sadness too. Many Angolans had died in prison and had missed the chance of ever seeing their parents faces again.

The news of Salazar's death spread throughout the colonies and the people of Angola were joyful.

Indeed, it was time to smile, because after four hundred years, many African countries had their independence. It was time to enjoy our independence after a very long fight. The battle continued, the Empire observed their defeat and started to leave the country. This was very serious for some of them as Angola was their country of birth. Unfortunately, they had to leave all their belongings behind, everything they owned was built on the back of slavery. This issue increased the number of white people who enrolled in the MPLA

No one in the world wants to lose their wealth, which they have built for many years, however, if it was built by slavery, this is different.

These were the white people, who were born or who had a business in Angola, rich or poor, this increased the fighting each day. The public burnt everything in front of them, factories, shops, flats, cars, farms and much more. Angola had the best economy in the Empire and Portugal became very poor, because they had lost it. The population destroyed anything they could and occupied many others. The black people moved from bad villages to the city centres, to houses and flats in attractive areas. Everything that they occupied, was built by them, when they were slaves, they could now start to enjoy their hard work. The black people never believed that one day they would have the chance to enjoy their work, however, anything can happen in this world. Some members of the Empire left their belongings to their best slaves or let's say their most trusted slaves. Because some of them believed that one day, they would return to Angola and get back everything that belonged to them. From 1960 to 1974, the world viewed many murders in Angola, because the black people claimed their country.

The MPLA announced that they were the only movement fighting for the independence of Angola.

CHICAMBA

The FNLA did the same in the Democratic Republic of Congo and the MPLA left the country. The Democratic Republic of Congo, supported the FNLA because they were the same kingdom.

Therefore, the fight was between the FNLA and the MPLA, but the victims were the employees who worked for the Empire and who came from the south of Angola. The MPLA supported the white and the mixed-race people, the FNLA supported the black people especially those from the kingdom of Congo. Tribalism was widespread, some people from the south tried to create the Republic of Nabuangongo to protect themselves in the north of Angola, but it was dismantled by the MPLA and they became part of the Empire again.

The MPLA, FNLA and UNITA, were waiting for a decision from Portugal as to what to do with the country. Sir Lúcio Lara, Pepetela, Paulo Gourge, Iko Carreiro, Rui Monteiro and many more white people were very influential people in the MPLA. The black people were not happy with Mr. Neto, and they were waiting for someone to support their cause.

In Portugal, Sir Américo Tomás, Marcello Caetano and many other members of the Empire, attempted to take responsibility for Angola, on the death of Salazar, but their plan failed, because the Empire's army controlled Angola. They had a plan and they wanted the negotiation to be in favour of the white people too.

Because of his wealth, Sir Américo Tomás, was forced to resign and his negotiation with the three movements in Angola, never happened. The Portuguese army governed with their air force, police and their commander-in-chief. They had their plans for what to do with Angola. They affiliated with the MPLA, because all of them would be poor if they had to return to Portugal. The top commanders in the Portuguese army, took responsibility for the negotiations with the MPLA, FNLA and UNITA.

The Empire's army nominated Almirante Sir. Rosa Coutinho for our decolonization. Because he had spied on the government of Salazar in the Democratic Republic of the Congo. He spied on the the movements of Angola and that culminated with his imprisonment, he was the perfect person from Portugal to decolonise Angola. The MPLA, UNITA and FNLA travelled to Portugal to negotiate, this took five days. On the 15th January 1975 in the Algarve, Portugal the agreement of Alvor was signed, for the independence of Angola. The agreement was divided into four copies, each movement received a copy, and Portugal now recognized that the three movements were ready to drive the future of the Angolan citizens.

Angola is a sovereign state, free from Portugal, and the three movements prepared themselves for the general election and especially for the battle for presidency. But the Empire knew, that each movement wanted power and the MPLA was perfect in their eyes, because they had many white members. However, the three leaders of the movements, without any knowledge of the Empire's thoughts, just signed the Alvor agreement, which turned out to be fraudulent. Many black people thought that Angola would be in their control, but this was not to be. The Empire, inside the MPLA, knew without a doubt that if the country had a general election, the MPLA would never win the presidency, because the members of the other movements could not understand why the Empire was still in Angola.

The Empire would have difficulty controlling their wealth, the Empire army in the MPLA was led by Sir Lúcio Lara, Iko Carreiro, Pepetela and many more white people. The Empire, inside the MPLA was desperate to rule the country again and this desperation disturbed them. The Empire army promised Dr. Neto, that he would be in power. However, the UNITA and FNLA sought this opportunity, but the MPLA was created by white people to protect their wealth. The FNLA and UNITA knew what the MPLA was doing, each movement before returning to Angola, went to see their sponsors. Dr. Neto went to Cuba to prepare his military support, he returned to Angola with the war machine of the Portuguese Empire army, ready to fight, as this picture shows below.

Dr. Neto, was already hailed as the president of Angola, without any general election in the country. This happened because of the numerous members of the Empire's army inside the MPLA. None of the movements had previously had the support of the military in this period and if the objective was to send the Empire to Portugal, why was Dr. Neto employing them now? This

question was forbidden and it is still being asked today. Maybe one day, people will talk openly about this and without any fear. Dr. Neto, was received in Luanda by the populace and the MPLA said; "no leader in Angola has ever received such a jubilant welcome". However, the MPLA were lying, as you can see in the picture below, the UNITA led by Dr. Savimbi, had a joyful greeting from the people in the province of Huambo, Angola.

Also, the FNLA with its former leader Dr. Roberto, was received in the province of Uíge with great joy, but sadly we don't have that picture. He was held in great esteem by his people in the kingdom of Congo.

The Empire nominated Mr. Neto, which spread throughout the country that he was the president of Angola, this left the FNLA and UNITA very angry with the MPLA. The FNLA endured difficult times, because of the death of Mr. Mobutu Seko.

The FNLA and UNITA tried to explain to the community why they took the Empire out of Angola and why they were inside the MPLA. This is very important for any society and unfortunately could destroy forever the MPLA.

The MPLA started to send into Angola, thousands of the Cuban army and Portugal, the MPLA and the Soviet Union sealed

ANGOLA HARD TIMES 1

agreements. They sent thousands of troops to Angola, to help the MPLA and the Portuguese government said; they were just going to help with the general election. After that, the army did not return to their country but remained in Angola as citizens and members of the MPLA. The Empire started to rule Angola again, with Dr. Neto as leader. Once again, the Empire controlled Angola and the black people were powerless. The members of the Empire's army were installed in all the Angolan departments and the black people lost their objective.

The Empire just wanted back all their wealth and the MPLA army isolated Dr. Neto, no one was allowed to speak to him without permission from Sir Lúcio Lara, and he wanted to know what it was about. The MPLA, made life very difficult for the black people and Dr. Neto was very sad for what he saw. The Empire did not agree with any black people joining the MPLA. In 1975 there were two MPLA groups, one for the white people and one for the black and mixed-race people, the mixed-race people favoured the white people. The MPLA for the black and mixed-race people was controlled by the white people or as they are more commonly known, the Empire. Unfortunately, Dr. Neto was practically useless, because of his white wife and the intelligence of the

Empire. The whole world knew that Angola was free, but this was of no use to the black people. Dr. Neto said that the agreement that had been signed was nonsense, but he forgot his secret meeting with the Empire army. He forgot that he had been made president, without an election and that the independence agreement totally opposed the Angolan black people. The FNLA and UNITA just watched what the MPLA were doing.

Dr Savimbi said "We can accept anything the Empire wants in Portugal, but when we return to our own country, we can change their laws". However, when they returned, they were still under Portuguese Empire rule.

THE FIRST DITACTOR

The MPLA led by the Empire's army in the background, decided to do what they wanted, fronted by a black person, Mr. Neto. The UNITA led by Dr. Savimbi, the founder and the FNLA led by Dr. Roberto also the founder, but behind them, was foreign interest that separated the country, because of their ambitions. Therefore, five days is not enough to discuss five centuries of domination, the MPLA violated the Alvor agreement, because of the Empire's army inside the MPLA. The first MPLA for the Empire in Luanda, had a secret meeting to prepare their next strategies, with the help of Sr. Lúcio Lara, Pepetela, Iko Carreiro, Rui Monteiro, Paulo Gourge and many more. Mr. Coutinho, the person responsible for the transition in Angola, did everything that he wanted to do. So, after the MPLA sent thousands of Cuban and Soviet troops to support the MPLA, the MPLA army controlled the province of Luanda and attempted to kill Dr. Savimbi and Dr. Roberto. The plan failed and on the 26th July 1975 the Unita and FNLA retreated. Thus, began the war, and the MPLA nonsensically blamed the FNLA and UNITA for starting it.

UNITA led by Dr. Savimbi, appeared in the province of Uíge in the kingdom of Congo and Dr. Roberto, appeared in the province of Huambo in the kingdom of Bailundo. In order to save our lives, we don't know where we could wind up. The MPLA did not succeed in killing Dr. Savimbi and Dr. Roberto, so they just managed Luanda, as the FNLA and UNITA had tried to reach Luanda to stop the MPLA and proclaim independence.

The Empire, Cuban and soviet-union armies became members of the MPLA, which controlled Luanda. The FNLA and UNITA were without an army war machine and were not as well prepared as the MPLA.

In Luanda , Dr. Neto, was forced to go to the square on the 10th November close to midnight, to announce independence on the 11th November 1975. At the same time on the 11th November 1975, the FNLA led by Dr. Roberto, proclaimed independence in the province of Uige and also Dr. Savimbi proclaimed independence in the province of Huambo.

This was very confusing in our society, each movement announced their independence separately, because of the MPLA.

Angolan history became meaningless, without the consensus of the population voting in Angola, war was inevitable.

General Iko Carreiro, planned to transfer the date of independence from the 11th to the 12th November 1975, because this was his son's birthday, he was born in Lusaka in the capital of Zambia. But, this was rejected by the other members of the MPLA. The three movements, MPLA, UNITA and FNLA, brought about our freedom, through their hostilities. Angolan citizens lost their dream of experiencing a general election and were once again under the control of the Empire. Many singers, writers and composers paid tribute to Dr. Neto, who was adored by the Empire, Cuban and Soviet-union armies, but the power of Angola, was in the hands of Lúcio Lara, Iko Carreiro, Rui Monteiro and Pepetela. Some of them had mixed parents or were born in Angola. The MPLA started their machinations, against the powerless black people of Angola. The black people had no idea of what the Empire had planned for the new State, or even themselves, they had not learned from their past. The Angolan black people had been ruled by the Empire for over 400 years and their weakness is well chronicled. The MPLA who were part of the Empire, Cubans and also the Soviet Union sent more troops to fully control the Angolan administration.

They became: governors, Mayor, army chiefs, Chief of Police, naval, air forces, and much more, and the black people of Angola just watched the Empire, once again, take control. They also recouped seventy per cent of their belongings left in Angola and laughed with Mr. Neto. In order for things to change the black people had to fight, but as the Empire held all the power, they had little chance. The Empire in Angola controlled everything, especially the radio and television, they decided on behalf of Mr. Neto what to do with the country.

At this time, UNITA disappeared and the FNLA attempted to fight against the MPLA, but they forgot they were also fighting with the Empire, Cuban and Soviet armies. The Empire army searched village by village, they killed many black people and put their bodies in a freezer. They then announced on the television and radio that the FNLA eat people.

When the general public saw the bodies in the freezer, they believed what the MPLA said, but of course this was untrue, the FNLA never ate people. This was propaganda invented by the MPLA.

Because they were dissidents of the Roman Empire, this was the same propaganda, which destroyed Cleopatra, many years ago.

Sadly, the illiterate amongst the black people believed that the FNLA ate people. In 1975 the FNLA was dissolved by the MPLA and lost the confidence of the people and also their international support. The FNLA without any defence disappeared and this affected the Kingdom of Congo, all because of the propaganda of the MPLA. The MPLA also tried to destroy UNITA, but its strategies failed, because when UNITA was defeated in Luanda in 1975, they disappeared and any accusations by the MPLA were discredited. The MPLA became the only movement in Angola and the Empire started to create laws. The MPLA called the country, the Republic Popular of Angola, popular means 'lands without law'. The MPLA created laws, according to what they wanted. The MPLA created the Angolan flag, which was the same as the flag of the MPLA, apart from a star in the yellow section between the red and the black.

The flag of the country had the picture of a gun, big knife, wheel and star. The gun represents communism or the Soviet Union, the big knife portrays when the Empire was removed from the country, however, they are still there, the wheel represents the development of the world and the star is for hope, which everyone desires.

The red represents the blood of the people who died for independence and the black represents the whole African continent. The objective of the MPLA was achieved, to have the same flag would confuse Angolan citizens. This shows once again, that those who have power can do anything.

The MPLA decided that the province of Luanda should be the capital of Angola, but in the Alvor Agreement signed by the MPLA, FNLA and UNITA in 1975, the capital of Angola, should be the province of Huambo, previously called New Lisbon. The MPLA changed everything, and they contrived a celebration, to celebrate the traditional date, which was based in the Judeo-Christian Bible and just for the satisfaction of the Empire inside the MPLA.

The MPLA created Angolan currency on the 14th August 1976, and they changed the name of the Angolan army many times. For example, EPLA (Excército Popular of Liberation of Angola) and also FAPLA (Force of Army Popular Liberation of Angola).

The MPLA feigned that Dr. Neto, was the father of the Angolan nation and that he was also the founder of the MPLA. But this was untrue, this notion was created by the Empire to glorify Dr. Neto forever.

The MPLA is still lying today, to all the new generations that grow under their rule.

On the 4th January 1961, the Portuguese military responded to the rebellion by bombing villages in the area, killing between 400 and 7,000 indigenous Angolans. National Heroes' Day is a holiday in Angola on the 17th September, the birthday of the national hero Agostinho Neto. This was not true because National Heroes' Day could be every single year on the 15th January, when the three movements, MPLA, FNLA and UNITA, went to Portugal and signed the Alvor agreement. Indeed, this is the date that the Angolan heroes among the kingdoms of Mucubai, Nhaneka, Cuanhama, N'guanguela, Bailundo, Kimbundu, N'tututchokwé, Fiote and Congo, which included the white people, formed Angola. The MPLA created the war in our society, because of its ambition to be in power and this started many disagreements among them. The first dictator of Angola was called António

Agostinho Neto. The MPLA had full control in this new country, but in the background, it was the Empire. The dictator Neto, was useless and was the first dictator in the world without any power. From the 19th Century the Empire carefully watched any black people who disagreed with them.

The Empire always checked if Dr. Neto talked with any other members of the MPLA and in particular with Nito Alves, Zita Tiago and Bakaloff. Because if Dr. Neto united with them, the plans of the Empire could be destroyed. The black people who were members of the MPLA, Sr. Nito Alves, Zita Tiago and Bakaloff, tried to talk with Dr. Neto but they were turned away and they were very worried, because Mr. Neto was oblivious. Nito Alves, Zita Tiago, Bakaloff and many more people, enquired into why Dr. Neto would not talk with them. They discovered that Dr. Neto was in the hands of the Empire. Nito Alves, Zita Tiago and Bakaloff understood that it was not the FNLA nor UNITA who started the war. Nito Alves, Zita Tiago, Bakaloff and many more members of the MPLA, discovered that the Empire was behind the suffering. The black people in connection with Lúcio Lara, Pepetela, Iko Carreiro, and many more white people agreed that the Empire should not be in the country. Angola was ruled by the Empire and not Dr. Neto. Nito Alves, Zita Tiago, Bakaloff and other black people, began to understand that it was the Empire behind the murders and it was their movement, the MPLA, who fabricated the fact that the FNLA ate people.

The FNLA and UNITA were innocent and had not started the war. The war was started by their movement, the MPLA, and they had to be very careful because they knew the MPLA was capable of anything, what happened to Dr. Savimbi and Dr. Roberto, was an example. But the deliberation came later because the Empire already had the country in their control and there was no one to challenge them. The black people inside the MPLA had no choice, they either obeyed or died. Nito Alves, Zita Tiago, Bakaloff and also more black people remembered the agenda of the MPLA and never supported it, their mission was to send the Empire back to Portugal. The black Angolans attempted to unite to stop the Empire controlling their country, but they were too late, the whole world knew that the MPLA had many black members, like Dr. Neto.

Nito Alves, Zita Tiago, Bakaloff and many more people, attempted to explain to the population what was going on. Dr. Savimbi from UNITA and Dr. Roberto from the FNLA helped but unfortunately they were defeated by the MPLA. Some MPLA members like, Nito Alves, Zita Tiago and Bakaloff and also more black people questioned the MPLA's actions but they were silenced by the Empire.

With the FNLA and UNITA in 1975, the population understood about the Empire. Dr. Neto, had no voice nor any power, he just watched what the Empire was doing with the black Angolans.

Nito Alves, Zita Tiago and Bakaloff attempted several times to approach Dr. Neto, without success, they never talked with Dr. Neto, because the Empire's spies prevented them. Also, his wife was a part of the Empire's intelligence, who controlled Angola.

Therefore, if anyone spoke with Dr. Neto, they could be in trouble, because the Empire's army knew Dr. Neto very well, and his belief in his people.

Lucio Lara and Iko Carreiro were leading the country, in the background was Dr. Neto, he was very sad at what was happening, but the Empire, Cuban and Soviet-union armies kept him under surveillance at all times. Dr. Neto was not permitted to move freely amongst the black people, he was only allowed to meet the people, that the Empire approved. Iko Carreiro, was one of them, he raised the hand of Dr. Neto, in all meetings, to show the world that he was happy.

Dr. Neto, just followed the rules of the Empire army, to save his life. He tried to find ways to communicate with other black people or other members of the MPLA, but this was forbidden. He also tried to make contact with Dr. Savimbi and Dr. Roberto, but the Empire found out and stopped him. Dr. Neto, was an idealist, if he talked with Dr. Savimbi and Roberto, all the plans of the Empire could be destroyed. Dr. Neto was very sad, because of the Empire spies, it was very dear to him. He could not speak with many members or the black people inside the MPLA, because he did not know who to trust. Nito Alves, Bakaloff, Zita Tiago and many more, started to complain about what the Empire army was doing inside the MPLA, with the Angolan black people.

As a result, Nito Alves, Zita Tiago, Bakaloff and many more people planned demonstrations in the streets, to show their concern. They believed that, Dr. Neto was a hostage in the hands of the Empire army, with the support of the Soviet Union. But the Empire planned again, to do the samething they had done to the FNLA, when they travelled throughout the villages, killing the black Angolan people and putting them in freezers, to say that the FNLA ate people. This time, with other members inside the MPLA, Lúcio Lara, Pepetela, Iko Carreiro and Paulo Gorge, they made plans to kill Dr. Neto and blame Nito Alves, Zita Tiago, Bakaloff and many more black people. But their plan was unsuccessful, however the Empire succeeded in planting a seed of doubt in the minds of the black Angolan people, regarding Nito Alves, Bakaloff and Zita Tiago.

Dr. Neto, with regret said;" these people will have no mercy" these words were very important, it gave the Empire army the opportunity to kill many members of the MPLA who disagreed with the Empire, such as Nito Alves, Zita Tiago, Bakaloff and many more black people. This holocaust is now called the murder of the 27th May 1977 and the death of thousands of people was called, the flowers of the Angolan nation, inside the MPLA. Because they were thoughtful with the black people, Dr. Neto, Savimbi and Dr. Roberto, had no power in the MPLA. No one was strong enough to challenge them. The MPLA became very powerful, and the massacre of the Angolan black people in the MPLA, pushed others to escape, to other countries around the world, to save their lives. Dr. Neto, viewed the murder of many black Angolans and felt very sad and alone, the black Angolans did not have a voice and they were unable to claim Angola back from the hands of the Empire.

The black Angolans spoke face-to-face with the Empire and challenged them. It was unsafe to speak about politics, if someone overheard, you would be in deep trouble.

These words are still true today, the Empire inside the MPLA, is untouchable. Dr. Neto, was very sad and started to drink too much, he also knew that one day, capitalism would rule the world.

Dr. Neto visited many provinces in the country and when he arrived in the province of Huila and saw many children, thin and malnourished, he asked himself why we fought for independence when our population was still dying through lack of food.

Also in the province of Cabinda, Dr. Neto said; "what we need is for the peasants and workers to have the power and not just production". These words were very crucial to him and when he returned to Luanda, the Empire knew that these words would open the eyes of the Angolan black people. Dr. Neto attempted to unite with capitalism through Dr. Savimbi, but without success. Dr. Neto knew he had to escape or he would be another victim of the Empire. If Dr. Neto could escape and unite with capitalism, this would destroy Communism, Leninism and Stalinism in Angola. Mr. Fidel Castro, advised Dr. Neto to be careful with the Empire inside the MPLA, he also advised him not to approach the Soviet Union for any reason, because they would kill him.

But Dr. Neto drank too much, surrounded by the Empire, his wife watched him slowly die.

Meanwhile, the black people in the MPLA don't have any power and the plans for Dr. Neto to escape failed. So, the Empire army with the Soviet Union poisoned him. They then took him to the Soviet Union where he died on the 10th September 1979. The Empire eliminated anyone who disagreed with them. The MPLA caught many black people and sent them to Cuba and the Soviet Union for military training. The country was independent, but none of the black people were in charge. Some of the Empire people left their wealth in Angola and returned after five years and got their belongings back. To protect their belongings, many people were killed, that was life in Angola. The kingdom of Dr. Neto was without power and lasted for only four years, the Empire had full control during this period.

So, Portugal sent more troops to Angola, and they sent some Angolan black people for military training in Cuba, the Soviet Union and other countries throughout the world.

THE SECOND DITACTOR

The MPLA in 1979 was clearly an internationalist movement in Angola, because their members were from the Empire who had dominated Angola for over four hundred years. The movement also included people from Cuba, the Soviet Union, Cape Verde and SãoTomé. Most of them were spies for the Soviet-union called the KGB, obviously with their high positions in the MPLA, they were white or mixed-race people. After the MPLA removed UNITA from Luanda, when they said that they ate people, They killed many Angolan black people, as we know from the holocaust on the 27th May 1977 and they also killed Dr. Neto on the 10th September 1979. Then, the MPLA chose a young man called José Eduardo dos Santos to be the leader of the MPLA, army and leader of the country. There were many black people in the MPLA who could have been made leader, but the MPLA trusted Eng. Dos Santos. He became the second dictator on the 21st September 1979, and was also a puppet of the Empire. The Angolan black people inside the MPLA, could only watch what the Empire was doing, they were powerless. The MPLA said that Dr. Neto had left a letter nominating Eng. Dos Santos, but this was untrue. This had been invented by powerful men in the MPLA; such as Mr. Lucio Lara, Pepetela, Paulo Gourge, Iko Carreiro and Manuel Rui Monteiro. It was evident that the young man was perfect for the job. He had no experience, he just obeyed the MPLA without question, as had Dr. Neto. He was also made President of Angola without an election.

Eng. Dos Santos signed many documents without consensus, which saw vast amounts of money being sent to Portugal by other members of the MPLA.

CHICAMBA

Five years after the disappearance of UNITA, they returned with great power and the support of the United States of America, South-Africa, Ghana, Zambia, and the United Kingdom. UNITA was back and was very confident that they had the ability to destroy the MPLA, and war began in Angola. Eng. Dos Santos had no idea what to do, he just watched and obeyed the Empire. The security of Eng. Dos Santos was led by Sr. Lúcio Lara, Iko Carreiro, Pepetela and Manuel Rui Monteiro. Eng. Dos Santos knew that his life was in danger, and Fidel Castro told him to watch his back and prepare his security team, if he wanted to stay alive. Fidel Castro knew what had happened to Dr. Neto, as Mr. Coutinho lived in Cuba and had told him everything. Eng. Dos Santos was advised not to trust the security team of the Empire, otherwise he would have the same fate as the people who died in the holocaust on the 27th May 1977 and also Dr. Neto. Angola was independent, but why were the Empire army still there?

This was and is the question that was constantly asked in our community, but Eng. Dos Santos only acted for the Empire. Eng. Dos Santos started to watch his back and changed his security team from the Empire army to the Cuban army. This unsettled the Empire army and the MPLA. The war escalated between the MPLA and UNITA, the first section of the MPLA attacked the second section, where most of the members were black people, and claimed it was UNITA. The MPLA, that had many black people, was lost and Eng. Dos Santos had to find a way to resolve this problem. He knew the failings of the MPLA but he needed them for his own safety. He started to make changes to the rules governing the MPLA, and this annoyed the Empire army and particularly Sir Lúcio Lara, Iko Carreiro, Pepetela, and Manuel Rui Monteiro. The Empire army were very worried as they saw more and more Cuban soldiers in Angola, as the security team for Eng. Dos Santos. The Empire army were very angry and they provoked internal fighting and also more battles with UNITA.

Many problems were left in the hands of Eng. Dos Santos, although he knew what was going on, to save his life, he had to keep quiet. UNITA attacked everywhere, trying to destroy the dictatorship in Angola and the Empire army was very afraid that they would lose their power to the black people. Especially Eng. Dos Santos, because he started it by dealing with Mr. Fidel Castro. Mr. Coutinho had explained all the strategies of the Empire army to Mr. Dos Santos, and he learnt many things. The MPLA and UNITA captured many people in the area and instructed them to fight in the war between them.

Men, women and children had to fight, and many were sent to other countries to be trained as soldiers.

Hopefully the children were just older people with small bodies. Each day the fighting between the MPLA and UNITA got worse, the Angolan black people were the victims of yet another war.

Many Angolan white people and mixed-race people were in Portugal unless they were officers in the MPLA, many said; they were not Angolan, no one wanted to die, even many black people fled to Portugal to save their lives. Angola witnessed great comedy as the members of the MPLA fought each other. Both sides betrayed themselves, the battle was only self-interest and the black people were slaughtered like animals. In 1982, many black people that were sent for military training in the Soviet Union and Cuba, returned. The black people were viewed as chiefs due to their superior training.

The Empire army had more experience and the MPLA attempted to kill Eng. Dos Santos, as they had Dr. Neto. This was unsuccessful, because Eng. Dos Santos, was protected by his Cuban army. Also, South Africa tried to get the province of Cunene on its side, that maybe, could be a payment from UNITA, if they could win the war against the MPLA. Thousands of Cuban troops were sent to Angola to protect the border between Angola and the country of Namibia, because the fighting there, was very fierce. This affected the province of Cunene, so it was a fight to the death. We were homeless in Angola without any chance to enjoy the benefit of independence. However, the fight in Angola was nothing to do with the black people, it was South Africa, the United States of America, the United Kingdom, Ghana and Zambia, on the side of UNITA, against Cuba, the Soviet Union and Portugal, on the side of the MPLA, but Portugal was on both sides. The Angolan black people felt deep sadness, caught between these powerful countries who fought in Angola, and they were the victims of terrible deaths.

From 1982 to 1985 the country was at war, the prize was the wealth of the country, diamonds, fish and oil.

Our spirits just disappeared in the sky carried with these powerful countries and the misunderstanding of mankind. The Empire army led by Lúcio Lara, Iko Carreiro, Pepetela and Manuel Rui Monteiro began to lose their power. The power was now in the hands of Eng. Dos Santos, who was protected by the Cuban army. The MPLA was divided into three parts; the MPLA of the Empire, who were trying to protect their wealth, the MPLA who defended the country against UNITA, controlled by the Empire and the MPLA of Eng. Dos Santos, who was watching his back. Sr. Lúcio Lara, Pepetela, Manuel Rui Monteiro and many more white people, in the name of the Empire, started to betray Eng. Dos Santos.

In 1985 Eng. Dos Santos, dismantled the regiment of the Empire army led by Lúcio Lara, he and his staff lost the authority to control the President. Many white people like; Mr. Pepetela, Paulo George and many more, left political life. The Empire army lost their power in the Angolan army, however, their ideology lived on with Eng. Dos Santos. If you saw a soldier of Eng. Dos Santos, you just ran and very fast, they would not say anything, they would just kill.

The army of Eng. Dos Santos was respected and very dangerous. He had to watch his back against the Empire and coup d'état.. The MPLA of Eng. Dos Santos, were just Cuban soldiers who became Angolan citizens.

From 1985 to 1989, the army of Eng. Dos Santos, went in all village schools and captured many children to send them for military training in Cuba. I can remember in my high school each year when the Cuban army fenced off or closed the school.

I escaped several times, because my grandmother every single morning came to bring me food at the school, traditional food like Fufu, boiled banana and much more. Whether Mrs. Vaenguela knew or not, which day the army would come, she saved my life and I can write this history. Each time the Cuban army fenced my school, my grandmother carried me on her back. She ran fast, crying as though carrying someone to hospital. She saved me from going to Cuba for military training. So, many chiefs or general military from the Cuban army captured school children, they took them to the Cuban army barracks to view. The children of parents or friends could be part of the army of Eng. Dos Santos, this was very dangerous and we are not allowed to talk about it.

Many of them once trained, returned to Angola and became high chiefs in the army or police, all around the country. This had never happened before, because during the government of Dr. Neto, the army was controlled by the Empire. This was the first time in Angola, that black people were allowed to be in better jobs; such as high chiefs, governor, mayor, commissioner and many other positions. During the government of Dr. Neto, black people were allowed to be chiefs but without any power or authority.

When Eng. Dos Santos got power and authority, he promoted family and friends from São-Tomé & Principe, along with Empire people from Cabo-Verde, they were welcomed in Angola, but the Angolan citizens were left behind. Eng. Dos Santos separated from the Angolan army, because of the coup d'état that may happen to him. Black people were caught to fight in the war, women, men, children and even disabled people, Mr. Kundi-Paihama said;" if you don't want to go to war, go back in the belly of your mother". Once we are born, we have never heard of anyone returning to their mother's belly. When men ran away to avoid fighting, the army knocked on every door and if you did not answer, they would knock the door down.

They were looking for men everywhere, checking each house to see if there were any men hiding. No end of families were destroyed by the war, many women did anything to save their sons from combat.

They would hide their sons in the bathroom with them and a polite soldier wouldn't force the door, but some soldiers didn't care, they went in and caught the men in the bathroom, roof or under the bed.

The men who refused to go to war were arrested, they were dragged along the ground to the military barracks. Only the black people arrived at the barracks with lots of injuries and some were already dead. All the army chiefs, especially the white people, sent their children around the world to receive first-rate educations. The UNITA did the same, they sent their parents for education and caught many people around the country.

Both movements, forced people to do their will, whoever refused to fight was killed and those who accepted may become high chiefs, with the grace of God.

THE UNITA IN THE CITIES

In 1985 the Soviet Union started to sense the arrival of capitalism; from the United States of America, which was introduced to the world. Capitalism gave business people the freedom to do what they wanted with their money. The United States of America showed the world the benefit of capitalism and its democracy, and they began conquering the world. It forced the world to adopt its system and opened the door for mankind to show their wealth. Many countries adopted this system and the rich people could enjoy the benefits. This change created many problems, because the communist regime had concentrated the wealth in those who worked for the government. In 1987 the Soviet Union showed many problems amongst their Empire, that affected Angola. This weakness by the Soviet Union between 1987 and 1989, gave full power to the United States of America.

UNITA, supported by the United States of America, was included in the decision to conquer Angola. The battle was called, the battle of Cuito Cuanavale, as we now know it today.

This battle terminated the lives of many Angolan and foreign people. UNITA forced the Cuban army to leave Angola in 1989, five years after the Angolan and Cuban governments signed an agreement, which was witnessed by the whole world. Unfortunately, the Cuban army became the Angolan army, because they had been in Angola since 1975.

Nevertheless, UNITA was supported by the United States of America, South Africa, the United Kingdom and many more countries. In South Africa and the United States of America, black people were excluded from society and suffered much abuse, an example of which is apartheid in South Africa. What interest did South Africa have in UNITA, did they want to create apartheid in Angola too? The country of Namibia was part of South Africa, the Cuban, Soviet and Portuguese armies fought hard to defeat the South African army in Angola and tried to force South Africa to grant independence to Namibia.

The MPLA and UNITA were respected throughout the world, but the situation of the Soviet Union completed the MPLA. Slowly the MPLA accepted the rule of capitalism and agreed to talk with UNITA, because they were supported by the United States of America and at this time nobody challenged them. In 1989 the Soviet Union crashed and the MPLA lost their strength and they allowed UNITA into Angola. Dr. Savimbi, with his movement UNITA, signed the agreement of Alvor on the 15th January 1975, along with the MPLA and the FNLA. The FNLA and UNITA ran away from Luanda on the 26th July 1975 to save their lives when the MPLA attempted to kill them. UNITA led by Dr. Savimbi, and the MPLA led by Eng. Dos Santos, signed the Agreement of Becesse on the 31st May 1991 and this event was watched by the world, especially, the United States of America, Russia, UN and Portugal. Fourteen years later Dr. Savimbi was back, brimming with confidence, that he could govern Angola. He had full support from the Unitied States of America. Therefore, Dr. Savimbi, with his movement UNITA, left the outback and moved to the city. This was the first time since 1975 that Angola had enjoyed peace and Dr. Savimbi appeared in the cities, with full support from the United States of America.

UNITA and the MPLA agreed to have their first Angolan election on the 29th and 30th September 1992. Other political parties established and they prepared their campaigns to win the election.

Especially the presidential election, that had been anticipated in Angolan society since 1975, by the UNITA, FNLA and MPLA. This had never happened before and this had caused civil war. UNITA showed the Angolan citizens, what we had never seen before or only viewed in films. Therefore, UNITA showed that we could talk face to face without fear, about big cars, motorbikes with four wheels, weapons and much more. This was the first time in Angolan history that we could enjoy each others company, especially those people who had parents on the side of both movements. It had been forbidden to be together, but now we could take this opportunity to unite. What we saw of UNITA was totally different from the lies that the MPLA had brainwashed us with. UNITA members were seen as human beings who had a connection with Angolan citizens, it made the community realize that the MPLA was not the only movement.

The UNITA opened the eyes of Angolan citizens and we believed that war would never happen again on our soil. Angolan citizens who lived in other countries around the world, returned en masse, happy to reunite with their parents.

The enjoyment was seen throughout the world, and after the suffering in Angola, people were happy for them. The rich people from the Empire who left their belongings in Angola, returned after eighteen years to reclaim them. Particularly, houses, farms, flats and shops. If they were now in the hands of the high-ranking military, they were not handed back.

However, if poor people were living in the houses, farms and flats, they were made to leave and were returned to the white people. From 1975 to 1992, the MPLA never encouraged people to register their property, so the goods were given back. If it went to court, the white people always won. The MPLA were forced to return property to the white people, by the directive of Portugal. This issue stressed UNITA and they called for any Angolan to give back belongings, However, they continued to turn up and claim their belongings, they came knocking on the door, interrupting many black people in the middle of resting, dining or making love. When they opened the door, it was the white people, back from Portugal, demanding the return of their house, flat or farm.

Many black people were very angry about the influence they had. The MPLA reduced the amount of property handed back, because people were complaining and they wanted their votes for the election. The UNITA brought new hope to the country and reminded Angolans to be on guard with the MPLA. UNITA advised employees to complain if their pay was poor, or delayed and also if they worked in bad conditions. This had never happened with the MPLA from 1975-1991, in order to stay alive in this period they had to keep quiet.

The UNITA brought new hope, the poor people in Angola saw the American currency, for the first time.

From 1975 to 1991, if the MPLA caught anyone with American money, they were questioned and had to explain where they had got it, who had given it to them and if they had any connection with the UNITA.

If they had parents inside the MPLA who had a high position, such as chief or were white, that was acceptable, but if they did not have any of these, an explanation had to be provided or they would die, because of the Soviet Union system that ruled Angola. Then, the UNITA changed Angola, so that anyone could show their American money. The MPLA was very worried, it was losing its power. The Angolans started showing that whether they were rich or poor, there would be no more trouble. Angola began to have free speech, this was made the first constitution of the country, there was no more to fear from the MPLA. From 1975 to 1990, the country was called the Republic Popular of Angola. The UNITA changed the name of the country to the Republic of Angola, no more popular. The UNITA allowed the Angolans to demonstrate, which worked well for the peace in 1991. The MPLA were very afraid of the UNITA, because it had the full support of the United States of America.

The UNITA was very powerful and Dr. Savimbi had forgotten that the MPLA had been brainwashing the Angolans since 1975. The UNITA just moved into the cities, completely forgetting that the MPLA's words were still in the minds of Angolan citizens. The UNITA told the citizens what had really happened in Portugal in 1975. Many Angolans had no idea what had happened in Portugal, it was very clear that the UNITA would win the first presidential election in Angolan history. The UNITA assured the Angolans, that the country was in their hands and they organized lots of festivals to win over the people. The UNITA started to follow members of the MPLA, to assassinate them. Members were killed but their bodies were never discovered, so others decided to leave the country with their families and move to safety. The UNITA attempted to control the members of the MPLA and what they were doing to protect themselves in the case of conflict. The MPLA did the same, but they were very afraid of the UNITA. In 1991, some important members of the MPLA supported the UNITA, because they wanted the MPLA to change. Change was needed and the UNITA continued to condemn the MPLA in their speechs.

The UNITA showed too much power and stopped people doing what they had been doing since 1975! The UNITA was called the democracy party but Sir Salupeto Pena, said Angola had too much freedom.

The clothes of Angolan women showed intimate parts of their bodies, however the revolution of fashion changed the world. The UNITA forgot they came and also, they were supported by the United States of America, who had a great democracy but did not agree with democracy in Angola.

UNITA brought democracy and wanted to stop the freedom, this was a clue for the MPLA.

UNITA was very respectable because it brought a new element to Angolan society, but sadly, the UNITA did not control their words. They were ready to win the presidential election, as they had experience of dealing with communities. The MPLA prepared many people to imitate the voices of the members of UNITA, especially the voice of Dr. Savimbi, they intended to sully their reputations. The professional voice imitators discredited the members of UNITA, the MPLA had played dirty since 1975. The UNITA had forgotten what they were capable of.

The parties prepared their campaigns, ready for the general election. The presidential election was the key event in Angola and was awaited with great anticipation.

The MPLA, FNLA and UNITA, were the parties who had discussed independence in five days. Which culminated in the signature of the Alvor Agreement on the 15th January 1975, in the Algarve, Portugal. After the MPLA tried to destroy the FNLA and the UNITA in 1975.

The campaigns for the general and presidential elections started in earnest. The MPLA misled its adversaries and contracted special people to steal the votes. The UNITA were sure to win this presidential election, however the country had been in the hands of the MPLA since 1975. The Empire army controlled Angola, whatever the power of Dr. Savimbi, but the Empire knew well the history of the black people. From the Romans to the Greeks, we understood when Cleopatra was betrayed by the Romans that this is the strategy of the Christian Empire in the MPLA. With full heritage of the Persian, Babylonian, Arabic, Greek and Jewish Empires.

The FNLA and the UNITA had lost their time to demonstrate to the Angolans, what really happened from the 10th to the 15th in the Algarve, Portugal. They forgot that the MPLA had controlled Angola since 1975 and had already won the election, without it even taking place.

The FNLA and UNITA, tried to show in their campaigns that they were fighting for all Angolans, but in their heart, it is thought they were more for the black people. Unlike the MPLA, who just looked after their own, since it was created in 1956.

The FNLA and UNITA tried to warn the black Angolan people to be wary of the MPLA, because many of the members were white people and the movement was very corrupt. Many of the Angolans were illiterate and did not listen to the advice, they had no concept of democracy. The people just followed whoever gave them food and drink. In particular, the speeches of Dr. Savimbi, were aimed more for the people and communities, he told them very clearly what he would do if he won the presidential election. The UNITA was capitalist with full democracy and the MPLA were more communist because of the influence of the Soviet Union. Dr. Savimbi's speeches, fully informed the people of his intents, unfortunately many of the people were uneducated and had no idea what he was saying about democracy. The first presidential election in Angolan history started on the 29th September 1992, with eleven parties. They were; Movement Popular Liberation of Angola (MPLA) led by Eng. José Eduardo dos Santos, Front National of Liberation of Angola (FNLA) led by Dr. Holden Álvaro Roberto, Union National of Independence

ANGOLA HARD TIMES 1

Total of Angola (UNITA) led by Dr. Jonas Malheiro Savimbi, Angolan Democratic Party (PDA) led by Dr. António Alberto Neto, Liberal Democratic Party of Angola (PLDA) led by Honorato Lando, Democratic Renewal Party led by Luís dos Passos, Social Democratic Party led by Bengui Pedro João, Front for Democracy led by Simão Cacete, Liberal Democratic Party led by Anália de Vitória Pereira, Independent Angolan Party led by Daniel Chipenda and Social Renewal Party led by Rui Pereira. The MPLA manipulated the results of the presidential election, and it was dishonestly declared that the MPLA, led by Eng. José Eduardo dos Santos, had 1,953,335 votes and 49. 57%. UNITA led by Dr. Jonas Malheiro Savimbi, had 1,579,298 votes and 40.07%. The Angolan Democratic Party led by Dr. António Alberto Neto, had 85,249 votes and 2.16%.

The FNLA led by Dr. Holden Álvora Roberto, had 83, 135 votes and 2.11%. The Liberal Democratic Party of Angola led by Sir Honorato Lando, had 75,789 votes and 1.92%. The Democratic Renewal Party led by Sir Luís dos Passos, had 58,121 votes and 1.47%. The Social Democratic Party led by Bengui Pedro João, had 38, 243 votes and 0,97%. The Front for Democracy led by Simão Cacete, had 26,385 votes and 0.67%. The Independent Angolan Party led by Daniel Chipenda, had 20, 845 votes and 0.52%. The Liberal Democratic Party led by Anália de Vitória Pereira, had 11, 475 votes and 0.29%. The Social Renewal Party led by Sir. Rui Pereira, had 9,208 votes and 0.23%.

Not all the parties won seats in the National Assembly. The parties that won seats were:

The MPLA received 2,124,126 votes, 53.74% and 129 seats, UNITA received 1,347,636 votes, 34.10% and 70 seats, The FNLA received 94,742 votes, 2.40% and 5 seats, The Liberal Democratic Party received 94,269 votes, 2.39% and 3 seats, The Social Renewal Party received 89,875 votes, 2.27% and 6 seats, The Democratic Renewal Party received 35,293 votes, 0.89% and one seat, The Democratic Angola-Coalition received 34,166 votes, 0.86% and 1 seat, The Social Democratic Party received 33,088 votes, 0.84% with 1 seat, The party of the Alliance of Youth, Workers and Farmers of Angola received 13,924 votes, 0.35%

and 1 seat, The Angolan Democratic Forum received 12,038 votes, 0.30% and 1 seat, The Democratic Party for Progress-Angolan National Alliance received 10,608 votes, 0.27% and 1 seat, The Angolan National Democratic Party received 10,281 votes, 0.26% and 1 seat.

These were the parties that had been elected in 1992 for the presidential and the National Assembly. UNITA led by Dr. Savimbi claimed that the MPLA had stolen his votes. This of course was true, and Dr. Savimbi, would have to wait until the next presidential election in 1996 and if the MPLA won again in the next election, it would be in 2000.

Maybe in 2000, it would be the turn of Dr. Savimbi to win the presidential election. The MPLA knew that Dr. Savimbi, would not accept the result. Maybe this was the time for the MPLA to kill him, they had tried once before in 1975. When they saw that Dr. Savimbi rejected the result of the election, they attempted to kill him once again. But the plan failed, as Dr. Savimbi was helped by the United States of America and war was started against Angola. Dr. Savimbi promised to pay for the weapons when he became the president, and he was despondent not to be in power. Dr. Savimbi rejected completely the presidential elections that had taken place on the 29th and 30th September 1992 and Angola was once again at war. Many people, especially the young, fled the country to avoid going to war. The people who had returned, intending to stay in Angola, their homeland, were forced to flee, luckily, they had dual nationality, so they escaped easily.

ACKNOWLEDGEMENTS

Firstly, I give my thanks to God or the creator of the universe, because of the many miracles that have happened and he is still in my life. I am always able when I feel the touch of God or the sound of his sweet voice. I felt the signs from God, but some were very difficult to understand, I asked God to tell me again what he meant. What should I do in this wonderful world? When I spoke to God, from my heart, he sent the signal again. I was to show in my books, everything regarding the true history of Angola, my country. It is difficult to talk about what happened from 1975 to today. We believe that circumstances of life sometimes send us to somewhere where our dreams may come true. Truthfully, this is me with the books Angola Light of Poet, PENXÁ VIVER Poeta, LONDINDI Poeta, ONGUTO Poeta and also this one, ANGOLA Hard Times 1. However, I believe that it was God, when I viewed the problems that had happened, I can say to myself thank you creator of the universe or God, for hearing your voice in this world. That he or she tried to let me know, that any troubles in my life that come from the mouths of mankind are very difficult to understand, to know what the creator wants us to do or say.

Many times, I missed the words of God and I said;

God forgive me for not understanding your way, forgive me for not paying careful attention to your signal and forgive me for my behaviour. In addition, some people envy us and try to destroy us, they don't understand in other hands all the registrations would be useful for somebody. Nevertheless, to build a country we need real history of life because it is very important for future generations. Writers like me, can show how dangerous life could be in Angola.. Dear readers, believe me, this is the moment that

I felt God speak to me, to send a message for a new generation. The MPLA is still attempting to confuse us, because it bears bad history and wants to control Angola forever. Nobody in this world, has the power, to control the earth forever. One-day the MPLA will disappear or weaken and give us the opportunity to speak. Indeed, remember I am a writer, the angel of God, who has the same vision as Joseph, who devoted his life, to go to Egypt. This is the history of my country, and the history is great, like Joseph who had dreams about his future before he went to Egypt.

No one believed what Joseph said about his dreams, especially his family, let us remember forever, this is our wonderful world where we can do our best to let new generations know about our country. Therefore, this is my history in the world and also in my lifetime, so I offer thanks to all my family, but there isn't enough paper in the world to mention them all. Also, my thanks to the Publishers who accepted my works, so believe me I am still with the kingdoms of Mucubai, Nhaneka, Cuanhama, Fiote, N'guanguela, Bailundo, Kimbundu, N'tututchokwé, and Congo, a part of me belongs to the physical and spiritual life of Angola.

REFERENCES OR SOURCES

www.club-k.net, www.angonoticias.com, www.angola24horas.com, www.makaangola.com, www.journalangolense.com

http://www.cphrc.org/index.php/documents/colonialwars/docang/85-1975-01-15-alvor-agreement-on-the-independence-of-angola http://www.prweb.com/releases/2015/AngolaLightofPoet/prweb12473230.htm http://www.globalsecurityorg/military/world/war/angola.htm

Source; African election database www.youtube.com it is where I checking every day to catch the events of my country that I viewing, hearing what happened in my country and around of the world.

Prescott L. (Ed) (2010) "The Voices and Texts of Authority" (AA100 Book 04) The Open University Milton Keynes,

Moohan E. (Ed) (2008) "Reputation" (AA100 Book01), The Open University Milton Keynes,.

Price C. (Ed) (2008) "Tradition and Dissent", (AA100 Book 02) The Open University Milton Keynes,.

Brown, D. R (Ed) (2008) "Culture Encounters" (AA100 Book 03), The Open University Milton Keynes,

Moohan E. (Ed) (2008) "Place and Leisure" (AA100 Book 04) The Open University Milton Keynes,

O'Connor, J. (Ed) (2003) Doctor Faustus,

Pearson Education Limited, Edinburgh Gate Harlow Essex, CM20 2JE.

Muldoon, P. (Ed) (2010) The Faber Book of Beats, contemporary Irish poetry lord Byron; selected poems.

New Revised Standard Version Bible, copyright 1989, Division of Christian Education of the National Council of Churches of Christ in the United States of America.

Carreiro, I. (Ed) (2005) Memoria, Editorial Nzila, Ltd. Rua Ndunduma, 308 – 2° Caixa Postal 3462 Luanda-Angola.

Marques, R, (Ed) (2011) Diamantes De Sangue. Corrupção e Turtura em Angola, Tintas-da-China.

www.ingramcontent.com/pod-product-compliance
Lightning Source LLC
Chambersburg PA
CBHW020019050426

42450CB00005B/544